A BEGINNING . . .

There is one major message that I wish to get across to you in reading *Odysseys of Light*. It is that there is absolutely nothing to fear in your reality and your world.

As one who has experienced hundreds of experiences out of my body, I know that all there is, is love! Hard to believe, isn't it? But, it is so true. There is nothing more true in the universe than this. All there is, is love.

Share with me my Odyssey through time and space, and allow yourself to open up to the possibilities that lie waiting. You, too, can experience the universe, if you allow yourself the pleasure and the joy! Meet and talk with your own spiritual guides and teachers, travel to different dimensions and planes of existence, go to different galaxies and talk with beings who are existing in a higher spiritual reality! Experience the unlimited being that you are, experience the Godness in yourself and in others.

My experiences are real. Having no desire to debate the reality of astral projection, I wish to open your reality to conscious contact with the other side.

Thought evolves and grows. *Odysseys of Light* represents the initial stages of growth, and is the first book in a series of eight. In order to fully appreciate who we have become, we must honor who we were in the past, which set the stage for the future self. As should be expected, *Odysseys of Light* represents who I was and what I felt at the time of its writing. Since that time, as creation continues to create, and the spirit continues to unfold and magnify, so, too, do thoughts and beliefs grow. *Odysseys of Light* is but the beginning. . .

Let's begin with my first experiences. At that point, confront your reality, take the challenge, and join me on the other side.

—Marilynn Hughes

Odysseys of Light

Adventures in Out-of-Body Travel

Marilynn Hughes

For information, write:

Hampton Roads Publishing Co., Inc.
891 Norfolk Square
Norfolk, VA 23502

Or call: 804-459-2453
    FAX: 804-455-8907

If this book is unavailable from your local bookseller, it may be obtained directly from the publisher. Call toll-free 1-800-766-8009 (orders only).

ISBN 1-878901-11-7

First Edition
10 9 8 7 6 5 4 3 2 1

Printed in the United States of America

To my readers, for sharing with me my personal journey with the love that this type of sharing requires.

It is true, in my own mind, that as we share this story of life together, we merge as one on a greater level, on a universal scale. I will know you in reality, as you now know me.

The writer's flight
The reader's mind
Merging visions
Bursting signs

Synergetic
Reaction pulse
Soul emerging
One with words

You and I
A creative burst
Of light from Heaven
And the Universe

Mere acquaintances
But Eternal Friends
Create your visions
And soar with the wind

* * * * * * * * * *

To Andy:

Only silence speaks the solemnity of gratitude I have for your soul. Through all walkways of life, your spirit has touched my own. And in the essence of our freedom, our lives still merge, bend and sway about in each direction of ourselves. All paths seem to lead back to one who supported, loved, and empowered me to soar, experience, create, and live my dreams. Though our lives are now separate, the gifts of our union are eternal and timeless.

There is no greater one
Than yourself, my friend

Whatever leads a path to start
May find the journey rare
Where love will last a lifetime's way
No matter near or far

Whatever pathway I may take
You've been a friend to me
There is no greater gift than this
You've always set me free

I loved you then, I love you now
And love will change and grow
That is why our bond as friends
Means so much more than you know

Perhaps it can be clearly said
With one more thing to say
I thank God for you, my friend
Each and every day

* * * * * * * * * *

To Marilyn Schweickhart, a traveler and friend who has walked with me many pathways, and loved me through it all!

THE FLOWER IN THE VALLEY

A flower in the valley
Blooms brighter than the rest
It's golden hue emblazoned
Petals flowing in the wind

The beauty of the flower
The wisdom of it's soul
Is apparent to all who catch the sight
As it shines forth from the soil

To all who see the valley
Their eyes meet with the rose
They may not stop, or even stare
But for a moment, their heart knows

Their spirits feel the gift
Of one who shines so bright
Their own soul feels the freedom

Lives change from just the sight

Marilyn, you're the flower
In the valley of my heart
Your friendship is a mighty rose
I cherish your love and light

* * * * * * * * *

A special thank you and heartfelt appreciation to Bob Friedman, for believing in me, one of the greatest gifts one can give or receive.

Thank you, Bob

There's a spirit in the cosmos
His name is Bob right now
But many names have held his heart
Many roles played out

I think of him a lot at night
While perusing from above
As one that I appreciate
And my soul must dearly love

He's given me the strength to feel
The power of my soul
The confidence and empowerment
To follow my highest path

Thank you, Bob, for all you are
You're held deep in my heart
For seeing all the good in me
And giving me my start

And thanks, again, must go to one
I remember in my soul
One known as Bartholomeuw
The higher self of Bob

* * * * * * * * * *

To all my friends and family, I love you very much.

* * * * * * * * * *

A special thanks to Mary Miller, my college English teacher who told me I could be a writer and urged me on. Thanks to Dean Rugh, my high school psychology teacher who brought the seed of truth to my vision gently, but with care, so as to allow it to grow into what it has become today. Both teachers seeded the path of my future in ways they probably don't even realize. A gift of knowledge is a gift of life! Thank you from the bottom of my heart.

* * * * * * * * * *

And a burst of light goes to all my unseen friends, who are seen, felt and loved deeply in my heart, and are a joyous part of my every moment. Thank you for giving me the gifts of all that I've experienced, felt and seen. And for the greatest gift of all, that is truth.

* * * * * * * * * *

My deep respect and reverence goes to Jesus Christ, Buddha, and all those who have paved the way for the spirit, for your courage, strength, and knowledge, to bring the truth, no matter the personal cost. I admire and love you beyond any capacity to express. May we all be as courageous as you!

* * * * * * * * * *

And,

TO THERESIA,

* * * * * * * * * *

And,

THANK YOU, GOD!

TABLE OF CONTENTS

PROLOGUE:
PATHWAYS TO ASCENSION: THE
OUT—OF—BODY EXPERIENCE

So many of us in the study of spiritual reality hear of the ultimate goal of connecting or reuniting with your "higher self." We've heard a lot about how it feels on the ground, and subtler explanations of tho depth of the experience. However, there is one aspect that we rarely hear about: what do the subtler aspects of ourselves *experience* while this reuniting process is going on.

Early on in my own awakening I began having out-of-body experiences, and my own reuniting with my higher self occurred while I was observing these other levels through out-of-body travel.

My experience began with what I call a vibrational state, where you are disconnecting your reality awareness from the vibration of your physical body to that of your spiritual body. The difference in frequency is very significant, thus, you feel a state of intensity of power. Experiencing fear the very first time, I thought I might be dying, but quickly realized as I rolled over and out of my body, that it was something else. As you disconnect with your physical form, you immediately connect with the mind of God. Unconditional love, wisdom, and understanding are easily felt as you separate. From this point I began the eight steps toward the reuniting with my higher self and ultimately bringing the ascension energy into my physical form.

Quickly, I learned that the process of reuniting with the higher self is a beautiful happening on these levels, and experienced very differently than in a third-dimensional union. And in observing those that I've worked with, I have found that the experience is very similar for a lot of people.

First, it is important to recognize that the out-of-body states are much more than a simple experience. Many of us have heard of experiences involving the process of waking up looking down at your body, or of near-death experiences with the tunnels and the light. Some of us have heard of other-dimensional realities and time travel. But few of us have looked at the full scope of what is really out there, and what is going on whether we choose to be aware of it or not.

Let me begin by mapping out for you a small sampling of my own experiences of the other side. There are tunnels that take you through time into past lives—a black tunnel with the light at the end. You often hear of this tunnel in near-death experiences, and my perception of why this occurs is because so many people at the moment of death also re—experience parts of that life in a movie-like sequence. What I call the corridor is the entry into the other dimensions beyond the physical. Having experienced literally hundreds of dimensions, it is my perception that there is no limit to this band of frequencies.

The plane we have heard tho most about is the astral plane, which overlaps the earth's third-dimensional reality and is lit as if by twilight. Some of the greatest misconceptions about out-of-body travel, in my perception, have come about as a result of information obtained in the astral plane.

Being the first place that one encounters in the out-of-body state, many have discounted the whole experience as having no worth. But, as I will show you, the astral plane is a necessary step in the process of awakening and eventually reuniting with your higher self in a complete, whole way.

We've heard so many times, "Go directly to your higher self, don't pay attention to any of those other things, like guides, etc." But the reality is that our higher selves, though always available to us, send energy down to us in the form of beings who can guide us higher, so that we can truly and ultimately connect with them. Though our goal and our destination is to be in constant contact with our higher selves, the process is often distorted and blanketed in dogmatic thought, because the goal becomes as misunderstood as the path.

In reality, our higher selves are on such a high band of frequencies, that in the process of coming together, we will go through other frequencies and levels of energy in order to bring enough lifeforce into our physical form to actually make true contact. This is not to say that when we communicate with them, they don't hear. On the contrary, it is that communication which brings the guidance and the helpers from other realms to us, so that we may incorporate a quality they possess, such as a deep understanding of oneness. Each will take us to a higher teacher, and each teacher IS an aspect of our higher selves. Ultimately, there will be a union, when all the energies are complete, and you've incorporated tho energy to be able to allow the powerful nature of this exchange to occur.

Eight major steps encompass this growth cycle (with the books in parenthesis that deal with each step), and with these steps, come continually more vast, brighter, more glorious worlds to explore in the out-of-body states:

1. Initial opening into subtler states (ODYSSEYS OF LIGHT)
2. Passage into co-creative energy (CRYSTAL RIVER FLOWING)
3. Process of surrender and trust (JOURNEY TO SURRENDER)
4. Rites of passage, initiation into the mysteries (ANCIENT TEMPLES LOOMING)
5. Re-emergence of karma (RED WINDS BLOWING)
6. The Angel phase (ANGELS TWILIGHT GLEAMING)
7. The gift of the Eternal Flame, completion (GOLDEN SPHINX EMERGING)
8. Pathway to ascension (THE BOOK OF THE EIGHTS)

INITIAL OPENING INTO THE SUBTLER STATES

Primary awakening begins, in my perception, with the very first glimpses of other realities through meditation, hypnosis, past-life regression, or out-of-body experience. It is the moment of the initial glimpse that the pathway for the individual soul actually makes the eternal connection that accelerates the seeker's growth immensely.

In the out-of-body process, the person will begin having experiences in the physical plane, while inhabiting their astral body, such as seeing their body from above, hovering about rooms, flying about tho surface of the earth, etc.

As the traveler becomes more attuned to guides, they will begin the early stages of the out-of-body process. This includes a lot of work in readjusting the consciousness to tho etheric form. Guides will work extensively with the seeker on re-learning movement, hearing, and seeing. All of these are now directed by consciousness, rather than a physical movement. Lessons in basic reality creation will be integrated, as well as work in reprogramming beliefs about the permeation of objects. This is to allow the seeker to become a fluid traveler in other realms of light.

Introductions to the initial teachers also comes about at this stage. Oneness is what will be touched upon first, and it will be shown to the seeker in a way that is very different than the earth experience of the concept. Blending will be introduced, which is the spiritual act of making love. It is experienced as two lights coming together, with a core center explosion of light, and the merging into one.

Core karma will be brought in, but only to be understood. Dealing with it physically comes later in the process. Introductions to special spirits who have connections with the karmic purpose of this lifetime will become very active at this stage.

Time travel is introduced, and the seeker may begin to experience the time tunnel, re—entering lifetimes that show the karmic pattern that they are here to overcome. Early stages of inter-dimensional travel will begin, as the seeker's guides begin the process of vibrational raisings that continually accelerate the energy of the form and the spirit to a higher level, thus, allowing higher and higher awareness in greater frequencies.

PASSAGE INTO CO-CREATIVE ENERGIES

As the traveler now begins phase two, the process of creation comes into play. Introductions to those groups of entities that work closely with that particular individual becomes common. Every one of us has special bands of alliances, groups of angelic beings working with us to bring the eternal through our physical bodies and into the earthly realms. Creation is a cooperative effort, and as the seeker becomes more attuned to these energies, he will find that everything becomes easy to accomplish, because he need only remain open to the frequencies of communication to retrieve the source which will guide him in the exact direction of his success. My own bands of alliances include many Bird Tribe energies, those energies of the ancient Native American peoples, and the Assisi Marauders, a group of five spirits who ride white-winged horses, directing vortex energy, a powerful creation embodiment.

The seeker is re-introduced to the many aspects of creation. Tools of creation, such as, The Causal Plane, The Vortex, the many realms of musical, artistic, and poetic energy that can be channeled through to the earth, and The Crystal Forest, a place in the realms of thought where the power of creation is amplified greatly. Amethyst trees, with rose quartz leaves, a clear quartz ground, and a golden river. Imagine, it exists!

As the traveler becomes a co-creator with God, a band of light is connected from the eternal to the earth-form. This light is the channel through which creation can now flow, and which tho seeker may travel to retrieve information about the creations he is bringing in. And the seeker can retrieve information about any and all details of the creation, including where to get material published, recorded, or displayed. How it will be done, what level of success it will have, and what kind of an audience.

Karmic agreements regarding artistic creations, scientific developments, or whatever your field of creation may be, can be identified in the out-of-body state. If you are a writer, You can discover who has agreed on other levels to publish your work; if you are a musician, who has agreements to produce and record your music; if an artist, which galleries will be expecting your work.

PROCESS OF SURRENDER AND TRUST

In gathering the knowledge you have attained, the empowerment that implies, and the initiative you have learned to take in creating your reality, it is a new energy altogether to bring in surrender. Balance is the goal of this stage of development, allowing the eternal timing of all things. . . everything in divine perfect timing.

In surrender, the seeker begins to acknowledge a deeper worth of self, working through issues regarding deservedness, self-love, and the beliefs in their own ability to create. Through surrender, however, the seeker enters into a state of trust, realizing that there is no creation that is not of God. And through this Knowing, one becomes aware on greater levels, of their self as a vessel of this creation. No longer is it an issue of self-worth, or the ability of the self. But the issue clearly becomes the all-powerful-divine-love, the creator of all.

Human beings are manifestations of an all-powerful divine love. Surrendering into love and the awareness of our union with all, becomes a more natural state. Previously, the seeker is used to the state of separateness, and it is in that state that one struggles to create. By breaking down these beliefs and entering the flow, the seeker learns that the only way of creation is a co-creation with God. When in this state of surrender, success is always easy.

The hardest task is to learn trust, and that everything manifests according to divine law, and that the timing is created by realities and understandings that we do not always access in this realm. We must trust, then, that the eternal is aware of all the multifarious possibilities and will bring creation to its highest potential at the exact perfect moment.

The ultimate realization is that all will be well, when you continue in the flow. Everything will happen at the perfect time, eternally, and we will never be without.

RITES OF PASSAGE, INITIATION INTO THE MYSTERIES

As the seeker is initiated into the mysteries, they will be taken back and forth in time to all the secrets of the ages, the Crucifixion, the Garden of Eden, the Pyramids, Noah's Ark, Egyptian mysteries, Greek mysteries, Native American mysteries. They will meet all the great seers who have attained immortality, such as Jesus, the Sphinx, the Messiah, Bird Tribe Indian spirits, Isis, Aphrodite, etc. They will be taken to see some of the most beautiful of spiritual symbols throughout time, such as the Star of Jesus, the Sphinx in its ether form, its purity, its truth, the Sun temples of the Incas, and the Pyramid Tombs of the Egyptians.

With each of these experiences, the seeker will be taken through a rite of passage. These passages are simply initiations into remembrance. They will also go deeply into all that remains of fear, and be required to transfer it into a deep understanding of love.

With that completion, the seeker is taken into the pyramid where he will make a choice. The *Book of the Eights*, the book of the immortals is presented to them, and accepting the book is accepting the gift and responsibility to reach for ascension in this lifetime.

Ultimately, the seeker will make his first uniting with his higher self. If you are female you will have a marriage with the female aspect of your higher self. If male, with the male part. This is the beginning of full completion and wholeness in the physical form. A reuniting with the other energy, whether it be masculine or feminine, will occur in the seventh stage.

At this point, where understanding of the highest truth on other levels has been attained, everything now seeks to manifest on the ground. All the knowledge and wisdom attained throughout the first four stages and initiation into self, will now hit ground level to be experienced and understood from the ground.

RE-EMERGENCE OF KARMA

Core karma is now beginning to manifest on the ground. Likely, the seeker will draw in fragments, other people, who represent the core karma that he has been shown from the first stage of light. And, once again, they will play their part with precision and grace, repeating the same patterns that have held you to the earth.

The challenge, then, is to begin seeing a higher perception of what has been misunderstood about love. What is the illusion that you have held onto about love, about truth, about these people and entities in your reality. Where was the love misunderstood, mistreated, misaligned, or mis-focused.

As the core karma hits the seeker's reality, he will find the same feelings from days of old resurfacing. Fully experiencing these feelings, and then realizing their true origin, their place of belief, is the purpose. Resolving the misunderstood love with these people in the seeker's life who represent the karma, is the goal. Knowing that they do love you, and their love is real—only disguised in illusion.

THE ANGEL PHASE

With the disguise, comes the angel phase, which is opening to the awareness of what is really going on with those in your reality, and the parts you play for one another, to show each other things that are necessary to incorporate in your knowing of truth.

In the angel phase you begin to see that oftentimes those who treat you the worst, love you the most on higher levels. As souls who have agreed to show you something difficult for you to see or understand in a way that can be perceived in a myriad of ways.

The Angel Phase marks the beginning of change in the seeker's life. Now wisdom hits the earth reality, sometimes with a great deal of power. Everything in your life that does not identify love, will be mirrored back to you. Anything that no longer works in your life, with your new understandings, will be challenged. And in this phase, a great deal of time and energy is given to re-evaluating all these changes. Which directions to take, what pathways to cross.

The ultimate question comes into play, "How far am I willing to take my spirituality: all the way, or some of theway?" In order to continue, it must be taken all the way, meaning that everything must be dealt with. No stone will be left unturned in the seeker's reality.

Different angel groups will be revealed to the seeker in this phase, those angel groupings that work closely with the individual. And, you will begin seeing deeper into the core essence of those in your life. You will find out who they are on the other side, their true self. Such as, someone who is mirroring to you a difficult lesson in trusting other people, may turn up to be one of your guardian angels in their essence. One who twists the truth and distorts wisdom, may be a Master Sage in the other realms.

THE GIFT OF THE ETERNAL FLAME, COMPLETION

This marks the beginning of a whole new series of rites of passage, which are actually more light and joyful, in essence, than the first series. As the darkest places in the soul have already been worked through and revealed, it is now merely a process of energizing and completing the energy of the totality of a soul in the earth-plane reality.

As the karma continues to hit the physical, and the seeker continues to deal with the massive change, they will be given secrets to make the pathway easier. Examples would be the energy of the Phoenix, the inspirer of change, or the Magic Lace, in essence the miracle of grace.

Major energy shifts begin occurring, preparing for the most dramatic aspect of this phase, the second marriage to the higher self. This marriage, however, is designed to incorporate the masculine or feminine energy that is not yet synchronized from the first. For instance, if you are female, you would now begin re-integration of your masculine energy. If male, re-integration of the feminine.

When these two energies finally do come together in union of one, the soul finds completion within ITSELF. And, as a walker of the eternal pathway, is content to walk that path alone, or with a fellow traveler. But there is no longer that "need" for completion by the opposite sex.

Core Karma usually still rages on through this phase, depending on the alertness of the traveler. As core karma, is the biggest block through the seeker's lifetimes, it is absolutely normal, to not see the highest truth the first time it comes into your life. But no need to be concerned, for as long as the seeker continues towards the life and the truth, it will re-appear until the seeker grasps the truth of this karma, and sets himself free of it once and for all. Oftentimes, this does not occur until step eight, when ascended completion emerges.

PATHWAY OF ASCENSION

Ascension energy becomes the focus now, as the seeker will receive energy raisings, vibrational raisings, and all sorts of energetic transfers to convert physical matter back to the liquid ether of the immortals. The seed of Ascension, the Gateway to Ascension, the Implantation process, all are energetic aspects that will be experienced along the pathway.

Atonement, however, is the major key in this phase. Everything must be brought back to love from the highest realms all the way down to the earth. Anything and everything that has been misunderstood about love, must be understood, resolved, embraced, and set free.

As a result of this need, the core karma, if unresolved, will escalate into a major mirror to the seeker. It can be a rough time, emotionally, for the most difficult love issues will be escalated, magnified, and thrown directly into your reality. Appearing overwhelming, sometimes the seeker can actually drop back a few notches in their eternal understanding. But this is okay, and sometimes necessary, to retrieve the ancient misunderstanding, and bring it higher and higher, until it is understood and let go.

When this phase is complete, the seeker will have the ability and the option to leave the planet at will. But many will opt to stay, out of service to the planet. Those who have truly passed completely through all these stages, oftentimes are the least likely to suspect, for they do not boast of it, and only speak of it to those who truly seek to know. It is not an accomplishment of the ego, but an accomplishment of love.

Beauty fills the life of one who has passed this threshold, however, because as a true bearer of the truth, freedom is yours! It is also true, that as long as you continue in your eternal path, wonderful things will be available to create from higher places.

Ironically, however, even ascended beings will sometimes disconnect from the eternal path and choose to live a life in the illusion—to experience the simplicity, or join another; but this can pull one back in evolution, and create even more karmas to deal with later.

It is only by choosing to constantly walk the eternal pathway, that one can pass through life creating only light and joy, and resolving issues as you go. No longer will anyone leave your reality without knowing in their heart your love for them. No more misunderstandings about love will remain misunderstood. Atone as you go, is the motto of the ascended one.

It is not that no more issues will come up, because they will, as anyone who is physical will continue to draw in things to understand. An ascended being brings those issues back to love, here, now.

Your physical body will actually change in subtle ways, and can often be described simply as more liquid. As the ascension energy continually expands into the particle energy of your form, your matter will actually change from a more physical substance, to a rapidly vibrating liquid mass, more fourth and even fifth dimensional.

At this stage, communication with spirits, guides, higher selves, and all those other realms, is commonplace, and continual. . .meaning, tuned into at will. Generally, however, the seeker will tune it out unless there is a reason, so as to avoid input burnout.

Again, at this stage, the seeker may choose to leave the planet at anytime. This book, called the *Book of the Eights*, again, because the Book of the Immortals, retrieved at the moment of choosing to seek ascension, is entitled as such.

SUMMARY

So the eight stages come together, forming a complete whole. But out-of-body travel will continue, constantly bringing insight to daily life situations, higher perspectives to complex problems, and loving solutions to angry words.

Out-of-body travel is much more than psychic phenomena, it is the process of reuniting with our higher selves, and ultimately, the Gateway to Ascension.

CHAPTER ONE
BEGINNINGS

My first experience out of the body occurred shortly after the birth of my first child. An interest was spurred, seemingly out of nowhere, in metaphysical issues. It started with archeology, then progressed onto other topics such as unidentified flying objects, reincarnation, ghosts, and ultimately my own spiritual journey.

Interested in astral projection, but not convinced that someone like me could experience it, I asked my guides to help me. Feeling a bit silly, as I had no contact to speak of, I decided to communicate with my guides anyway, affirming to them that I *knew* that there was so much more to the universe than I was currently aware, and I wanted to learn about it. As you know, we all have spiritual guides who work with us on our own journeys through life, helping us to learn what we chose to learn before arriving here. Whatever blocks and fears I had, I was determined to work through, and I let them know that. Knowingness was something I wanted to have, not just faith. It was important to me to experience my unlimited self. . .One morning, I did.

Preparing to get out of bed, I turned to get up. Suddenly, my body began to vibrate, not my physical, but my etheric body. At the time I did not know the difference. It felt like my physical body was literally going into a massive seizure, the vibrational force was so strong! Terrified, I felt the vibrations continue. My body felt what could be termed "beyond numb." It sounded as if my body were surrounded by jet engines. I later learned that these were the sounds of the astral plane. I lifted my arm, as if to somehow break the strange condition. My hand lifted ethereally out of my body. A light image, glowing like a sparkler, came out in the shape of my arm. My physical arm stayed put. I was intrigued. It was time to experiment.

Remembering my affirmations to my guides, I decided it

was possible that I could be experiencing some sort of out-of-body experience, so I rolled over to see what would happen. My etheric body rolled out onto the floor and bounced upwards towards the ceiling, and then through it. Looking down at the room, I became frightened. The fear overcame me, and I quickly jumped back into my body.

The terror I felt cannot be overstated. My fear was of the intensity of the vibrational state. Since I was not expecting such intensity, the fear lasted several days. I hesitated to go to bed, as it might happen again, but calmed myself by talking with my guides and asking fervently that they help me to experience this without fear.

Even when you don't hear your guides, they always hear you. I spoke with them in my mind every night before going to bed, confirming the biblical saying, "Ask, and ye shall receive."

Everyone astral-projects at night, including you! Some people remember it consciously, others remember it subconsciously. Know that your center of being is not in a shell, know that you are free. Desire to experience the freedom of your spirit, and you will.

While trying to get out of bed several weeks later, I saw a beam of bright white light seconds before it permeated my being, spurring the vibrational sensations that occurred before.

A distinct difference was immediately clear, however: I felt no fear. My being was swept in a joyful sensation of love and peace! An incredible sense of knowingness came to me, what I now term the connection to the God-mind. In my new state of awareness, there was only love.

Another presence became detectable, as I felt the essence of my spirit guides behind me. Their radiating beings began to slowly lift me out of my body, their lights shining around me. I felt so safe.

Floating above my body, I looked below. There was no fear, but a strong sense of the separation from my physical form. The feeling was ominous, as I had never imagined viewing myself from somewhere other than my body.

The engine-like sounds of the astral plane could be felt as well as heard. My sight was coming from my entire essence, rather than from the vantage point of two physical eyes, and my hearing was the same. It felt unusual.

My guides led me back into my body, and they were gone to my conscious awareness.

All there is, is love. God does not judge, as his vibrations are too high to even consider such a thing. I now *knew* in my heart that there really was nothing to fear in the spiritual realm. God is unconditional love, and it is our goal to strive to reach that state in our physical bodies, difficult as it may seem.

One problem was adjusting to my astral faculties. My vision needed help. Speaking to my guides about this problem, I asked for their help to better understand how to utilize my astral sight. When you disconnect from the physical body, you see and hear from all locations of your consciousness or being. As I was more used to physical senses, this would have to be re-learned. Time and patience were of the utmost importance.

The baby was napping, and I took advantage of the opportunity to get some shut-eye. I rolled out of my body after the vibrations began and tried to move around the house. Unable to leave the room, I realized I had a block.

In the corner, my baby's essence happily hovered. Happy to see her, I sent her a message of love, and she acknowledged. Wanting to do more, but unable to manipulate any significant movement, I returned to my body and awoke.

Astral movement, like astral sight, is consciousness_ oriented, rather than body-part-oriented. I would try to move by walking, or even wading like I would when swimming, but I was not in a physical body, thus, physical functions were useless. I asked my guides for more information.

Astral movement is in the mind. All astral function lies there. You must **will and think** movement. You can go anywhere simply by thinking of the place...easier said than done, but with a little effort, a piece of cake.

Another anecdote I learned was that babies, in their quest to make the transition from astral being to physical being, project. This is why they sleep so much. The transition is sometimes difficult.

The next experience included a little lesson.

While I was taking a nap in the afternoon, the vibrations started. The vibrations were very strong, but I could not seem to lift out. Willing astral sight, I was determined to get to the bottom of this. But a holographic image of my husband, Andy, was sitting on me, blocking my exit. Sending him thought-forms, which are telepathic messages which include thoughts, pictures, and feelings, I wanted him to get out of my way so I could fly! The image of Andy laughed, and moved to the calves of my legs.

Finding myself getting more and more agitated, I began to wonder about the meaning of this experience. I had been putting a lot of pressure on my husband lately about his own spiritual growth. He wasn't ready. Just as Andy was inhibiting me in the holograph, I was inhibiting him. Pressure was only turning him away, and the anger I felt at the holographic image could easily be the same type of feeling Andy could be having for me. I understood. I stopped fighting the image and willed the vibrations to cease.

On the astral plane, thoughts are things. You create whatever reality you truly feel by your thoughts. I could have confronted the image of my husband, and permeated the illusion. But I was still thinking in physical terms, and allowed the image to control me. It is difficult to break a belief system which tells you that you cannot permeate things. Well, you can.

Many of you may choose to experience negative entities. This is only your own fears coming to life. If you confront what you create on the astral plane, it will simply disappear, as they are illusion. Fear is illusion, as all there is, is love. You can create whatever reality you desire, and if you are fearful, you may create a very scary illusion. You create them because of your unrealized fears. What you create, you can also destroy. Confront it. Ask your guides to help you understand things from the spiritual realm, rather than from the physical. As it is only in the physical illusion that we create fear.

With every projection, you should try to do something new. Take your time, and allow yourself to develop at your own pace. Your guides will not overwhelm you.

You will receive guidance from your spiritual guides in the

astral state. In the astral state, you are also connected to the God-mind, thus, you have access to much knowledge and love. Allow yourself to accept that information, and discern what is important to you. You have more power than you realize, as literally the power of the universe is at your disposal. Tap into your higher consciousness, and grow!

The vibrations began, and I rolled over to get out of my body. Moving around the room, I noticed the window. It was early morning, a perfect day for a flight outside! Going towards the window with a little bit of hesitation, I permeated the window and found myself hovering outside. A slight resistance was felt as I went through the window, due to my own belief systems about physical reality. When I removed that doubt, there would be no resistance.

Hovering outside, I noticed the constancy of temperature in the astral body. No hot or cold, just a constant comfort.

I began flying down the street, through the backyards of my neighbors. I came upon a big dog. He immediately saw me and began to bark. Forgetting my astral state, as I felt so normal, I began to fear that my neighbor might see me hanging out in her backyard and get angry with me. She came out to yell at the barking dog, and looked straight at me, and through me. This was the first time I had stood directly in front of someone without being noticed, and it felt strange. As you feel no different than you would in your body, it is quite amazing.

A thought of my home came to me, and I instantly returned there. For some reason, I then thought of the home I grew up in and it appeared in astral form in front of me. Inside there was no furniture, just an empty shell, but I traversed the thought-form anyway. Suddenly, information on the creation of reality began to flood my consciousness. We create our own reality on both the spiritual and physical planes. Every thought we send to the universe manifests somewhere, just like the house. Surround yourself with love, and love will come back to you. And, surround yourself with negativity, and you will receive the same. Willing the house to disappear, and re-entering my present abode, I went into my body and awoke.

The recognition, or lack thereof, was significant to me in

this experience. You feel the same when astral projecting, and thus, expect recognition. But, you are an entity when you astral project. To those on the physical plane, who do not realize that they are just ghosts in a body, you are not the same.

Every thought you have manifests in another dimension. These thoughts build up and hang around you, so maybe you should consider incorporating more positive thoughts into your repertoire.

Surround yourself with positive people, too. Energy is easy to pick up on. If someone is very negative, there is no reason to allow that negativity into your reality. You create it all, so take responsibility for what you allow into your drama. Some people say, "I don't know what it is, but I just don't like being around that person." You know what it is. They are emitting negative energy. Likewise, some people just attract others to them, because they are so positive. Allow yourself the part of God that you are, the reality that makes you feel good.

The vibrations began and I consciously **willed** myself out of my body. Whirling through the window and onto the street, I saw that nighttime was in full force. Despite this, the astral plane was lit like twilight. Other entities were hanging around the astral plane paying no attention to my presence, but soaring twenty feet above the street. I was well aware I was now a part of this dimension of reality. Peaceful feelings could be felt emanating from everywhere.

Continuing to feel more excited, I began wondering if I could just go anywhere I would like...perhaps, to see a friend of mine in Texas. In a split second, or less, I found myself flying along an old country road with farms and plantations. Big, stately, old mansions stood tall amongst the farmland. I permeated the road, and traveled with part of my being in the road, and the other part slightly above. A sudden fear hit me, if I were really in Texas, how would I get back home?

A second later, I was back in my body, disappointed that I had allowed my fear to shorten my experience.

This was the first time I had seen other entities, and the first time I had gone on a significant trip. I was intrigued by the lighting of the astral plane. It was lit as if by twilight...not dark, and not light.

Again, I spoke with my guides about helping me with my

fears. In order to continue to move onward, I needed to work through all of these things.

Relaxing comfortably when the vibrational feelings began, I had no desire to leave my body, as I was feeling so utterly absorbed with the God-mind connection. All I wanted to do was absorb this feeling of total love and peace.

My spirituality was being explained to me. The key to spiritual evolvement is to live in the now. It's not what you are, it's what you become! The past is dead: don't live in it any longer. Do not judge yourself or others, just learn from life. Search for the positive in yourself and others, and when you make a mistake, don't dwell on it, change it. Admit to yourself your own imperfections. Imperfection lies in the inability to recognize such, not in having some.

The connection to the God-mind carries so much valuable spiritual insight which cannot be explained in earthly terms. It could be described as similar to turning on a light. With electricity, you plug a lamp in, and there is light. Rather amazing and complicated if you are not an electrician.

I was feeling peaceful. The vibrations ceased and I returned to the conscious state.

Several weeks had passed before that experience. We were moving to a new home and I was now allowing a lot of space in my mind for spiritual matters.

An important lesson was learned: to feel comfortable with my role in life. What does a woodcutter do once he has gone to the mountain and been enlightened? . . . He still cuts wood! No matter what you do in your life, it can be done more spiritually. Spirituality is a way of being, not something you do. Take care of you, do not try to save the world. If everyone focused on their own inner growth, there would be no need for rescuers. And I still had a long way to go to reach the proverbial enlightenment.

Vibrations began and I separated, entering a different dimension that I had not yet encountered. I leapt back into my body in fear. The black void I went to was different and new, thus scary. I willed myself to go back, but in the void, fear overcame me again. Back to my body. This time I was so determined to go back and experience whatever there was to be experienced, and I felt that determination from every corner of my consciousness. Back to the black void, I went.

Passing through the black void, I found myself in yet another dimension. Entities there recognized my presence, and it was obvious that they knew I was an astral traveler, and not dead. Feeling the dimension and looking around, I felt no more fear and just waited.

Moments later, a friend of mine who had passed away several years earlier had appeared. He was my brother's best friend and had died in a car accident. He spoke to me as if there was something important for me to know, but I was so overwhelmed to see him that I blocked everything he was saying. Laughing a bit, my friend hugged me in understanding and went on his way.

Passing through the void, I hoped we would meet again. I awoke.

This was a turning point for my fears, as I confronted them and didn't allow them to interfere with my experience.

Connecting to the other realms was becoming easier and easier for me. I was beginning to remember, as it is really the natural way of being. After all, we have been doing this ever since we began our existence thousands of years ago!

Materialization was the next step in my journey.

After leaving my body, I went to a very large and beautiful mansion in Europe. As an observer, I noted that the language being spoken was not English, and sounded European. With the connection to the God-mind, however, I could understand them quite well.

A woman lived in a big mansion all alone. I knew her to be my mother from a previous lifetime; however, this was her present lifetime which had no connection to me at all. She was widowed and bitter; the sadness she was feeling was evident. She had a boyfriend who was at the house while I was observing. In a house next door, her son lived. A tall middle-aged man with brown hair, completely bald on top, with hair remaining on the sides of his head. He was wearing a blue polyester suit. Realizing that this guy was my "brother," I went over to him and tried to make him aware of my presence, but to no avail. I had, once again, forgotten my immaterial nature. For only a second, he confusedly looked my way as if he knew something was there, but then he shrugged it off and turned away. He could not see me and I accepted that fact.

Flying about, I found myself in a filthy slum somewhere not too far from the first place I visited. Everything looked gray and dirty, and it was not a pretty sight.

A barroom in this ghetto was my destination, and I flew in and immediately noticed a father and son, who apparently owned the place and lived there. The brunette, and slightly pudgy boy of about eight years was not happy. His father, a skinny brown-haired man was getting rowdy with his friends, and it seemed that this was a regular occurrence. The son got very angry and ran over to his father with a pitcher of beer, pouring it all over his head. Responding in a fit of rage, the father chased the child around the bar to a back room, having serious thoughts about beating the child. I knew I should intervene. Floating in-between the two, I sent thought-forms of love to the man and his child. Universal love and acceptance poured through me and into them. Suddenly, the father calmed, and began to laugh. Putting his arm around his son, he commended him for expressing his anger and having the nerve to pour a pitcher of beer on him. My intervention was finished, and I flew from the scene.

Flying high up in the night air, I felt so much joy and peace, I truly wanted to share it! As I was soaring over a small clearing in a wooded area near a car dealership, I noticed a man sitting on the hood of his car staring into the night sky, searching for answers. A rush of energy and desire to share with this being came over me and I materialized into a white wispy form of myself and circled the sky sending the message of eternal peace and joy. "There is no need to fear God, for he is a loving being. Experience God within yourself, by journeying inward." I received an affirmation that he had heard the message, though I do not know whether it was conscious or subconscious. Sometimes beings will hear a message with their subconscious if they are not ready to consciously hear it. Finished with this locale, I flew away.

Following some train tracks, flying with the breeze, I heard the sound of a train coming. Great fear overcame me, would I be run over by the train? I flew faster towards a train station that was teeming with people. I wondered what all the fuss was about, and noticed a small bakery that everyone was crowding around. Changing my vantage point to behind the counter, I observed the event. I picked up a spoon, and was startled when a woman came into the area looking for it. She was angry, as she thought the peasants had stolen it, again. Laying the spoon back down, I decided to go home.

Flying through the air in a small suburb, I decided I would drive home. Forgetting my astral status, I created a thought-form car. While driving down an interstate, I realized that not only was this highway completely unfamiliar, but the other cars were permeating mine. Getting a bit angry at being cut off like that, I suddenly realized that I was astral, and they could not see me or my thought-form car. I quickly disposed of that reality and willed myself home.

Upon my return, I realized that I had been gone for about two hours, the longest experience to date. This was my first experience doing conscious spiritual work with others on the astral plane. Little did I know that I would do so much more in the very near future!

Another exciting adventure occurred when I had my first past-life experience out of my body! Vibrations came and I willed myself out. A large black tunnel with a light at the end was in front of me and I felt absolutely and totally drawn to go into it. Moments after entering the tunnel, my spiritual entity was dropped into the body of a soldier doing battle behind a rock barricade. The other side was a mere one hundred feet away. This seemed to be an old war, but I could not place the time period. It could have been the Civil War or hundreds of years before!

Our captain told us that we would shoot at each other for a certain stretch of time. Then, we would all count our wins and losses, and it would be over, at least for a few hours. For just a moment, I was calm and accepted it as something I had to do. Then rage overcame me and the idiocy of this act became very clear. Thoughts of the injuries I could sustain or inflict went through my head, and a terrifying fear came over me. I was truly experiencing the absolute terror of a man in battle.

Suddenly, I screamed out, "We don't have to do this, we don't have to kill each other! They can't force us to pull the trigger! This is not an acceptable way to work out disagreements!" I walked away and three men on my side of the battlefield followed me. Holed up in a nearby home, we heard the shooting, the screams, the carnage, the dying, the suffering, the barbarism, and we all began to cry uncontrollably.

The emotional pain was so intense. What a disgusting excuse war was, and where were our world leaders now? I was overwhelmed with grief and emotion. My guides quickly snatched me out of the body and led me through the tunnel home. I awoke very distraught.

A very personal experience, felt in a very personal way. I'd always known the futility of war, but now I truly understood what it meant to be in battle.

At this point, I am going to take a short break from my own experiences and give you some information on astral travel.

What you need to do to reach a state of readiness to remember your own experiences, and what you may experience once you get out of your body.

Afterwards, I will lead you on an ever-unfolding odyssey flight into the world of higher vibrations and love. If you think what you have read to this point is exciting, wait until you see what wondrous experiences lie waiting for those who are patient and persistent enough to master the art of astral projection. We have only begun, the best is yet to come!

CHAPTER TWO

GETTING THERE

We all have had astral experiences at night. Some of us just don't remember those experiences consciously. If you have had flight dreams, those were astral experiences that you remembered only partially. Your dreams hold the key to your fears: pay close attention to them.

Why is it important that you remember your astral experiences? Well, it certainly will not be the end of the world if you do not. But your astral state is a natural state of being, and if you do not remember it, you are losing half of your life experiences. Needless to say, a very exciting half, as it is your astral life that opens doors in the physical realm. Can you imagine having access to your guides, being able to talk with them one on one about your problems as you do with your closest friends? Well, you can, and you will! There is no life experience that can compare with out-of-body experiences, as experiencing that state is experiencing yourself in your unlimited form. You can travel to other lifetimes to understand the present significance, you can meet your guides and teachers, you can help with literally thousands of jobs on the astral plane, including the disaster crews, lost souls, subconscious work, astral support groups, and even helping beings in their transition between lifetimes. There is so much to experience on the astral plane, that the only thing I can say to you is that if you desire it, GO FOR IT! If you don't desire it, than finish this book and see if you feel differently.

Some people ask me if it does not get tiring having conscious memory 24 hours a day. NO, NO, NO! I feel more rested when I return from an astral visit than I do when I inhabit my body. This is due to the fact that when I leave my body, the body has an uninhibited sleep pattern. When I am in it, my body deals with the spirit's interference, thus getting less sleep.

As far as I am concerned, the astral state is a natural state of being, and if you are not consciously experiencing it, why not try? You have nothing to lose and the universe to gain!

I have compiled a short list of things to start doing, if you're not already doing them. Remembering, that the state of being is what is necessary to reach conscious recall.

The goal of what you are about to do is to ultimately reach a level of self-love and self-acceptance, and universal-love and universal-acceptance.

1. Spend one hour a day completely alone with yourself! No television, radio, books, meditation tapes, just YOU.
This may be awkward at first, but allow yourself to begin getting to know you. Become your own best friend. You might be uneasy spending time with yourself, as you may be afraid of what you might find. Find out who you really are, bad and good. Forgive yourself for your imperfection. Many of you spend hours talking about metaphysics; now you are really going to do it. You are a fun person to be with, enjoy your own company! Spend some time with your very best friend in the world, YOURSELF!

2. Every morning upon waking, spend five to ten minutes bringing dreams back consciously. Keep your eyes closed and think of whatever you can remember, even if it is only one detail at the tail end of a dream. Note the feelings you have upon waking as emotions and feelings are all that exist in the spiritual realm, and give great clues. Write down what you can remember, and start deciphering the meaning. That is how you can find your fears, you are the detective!

3. Talk to your guides throughout the day. They are your constant companions so involve them in everything you do. Regard them as friends, and they will be the best friends in the world to you. Express your desire to astral project consciously, and truly feel that desire. The emotion behind the asking is what creates the reality you desire. Feelings are all that exist in their world, and empty words mean nothing.
Never forget to thank your guides for anything they do. No matter how small, gratitude is important. They help you out of the goodness of their hearts, so let them know how much

they mean to you, and how grateful you are to have them. Everyone likes to be appreciated, even spirits!

Pay attention to their presence. They may do any of a number of things to make you aware of them. Acknowledge everything they do, so they will know you got the message:

> Seeing colors when you close your eyes
> Noises around the house
> Movement of objects in the house
> Unexplained household happenings

Pay attention to the wind and all things of nature. What have you failed to notice in the past? Notice the beauty in a flower or a child. What about the beauty in all of us who are confused about reality, the beauty of their unrealized desire to know the truth, and the beauty of this entire illusion. Start paying attention to everything around you in a more involved way!

4. After speaking to your guides at night, go to sleep meditating on love or oneness. Allow your mind to wander into its own understanding and experience of love, and enter into a questioning state of wonder about love. As love and oneness are all that is on the other side, your guides will happily oblige your interest. Remembering that you must truly feel that desire to learn. Do not be so arrogant to assume that your life is just too hard and complex to focus on just love or oneness. If you truly understood their vastness, your life would not seem so complex. You would be in a state of acceptance, and that is the goal.

Lastly, work on remembering your fears. I have listed some that you may not realize you possess. The supply of fears are endless, this list is just the tip of the iceberg. Remember, all fears are a result of an illusory feeling of separation from God; you must find them and put them to rest.

FEARS:

> DEATH (You cannot die from astral projection.)
> DEMONS, HELL (They do not exist, all there is, is love.)
> NOT BREATHING (Astral bodies don't breathe.)

GHOSTS (All you are is a ghost in a body.)
THE STRONG ENERGY (The energy force is very strong.)

LOVE (Afraid to feel true unconditional love.)
CHALLENGING YOUR REALITY (Your truth could be wrong.)
CONFRONTING YOUR EGO (Need to hold on to your drama.)
CONFRONTING YOURSELF (Admitting imperfection.)
BEING ALONE WITH YOURSELF (What will I do?)
THE UNKNOWN (Will I get lost in the vast universe?)

BLOCKS
LACK OF SOLITUDE, INTERRUPTIONS
NOT EMPTYING YOUR BLADDER
FILLING HEAD WITH GARBAGE (TV violence, ego stuff)

NOT IN A STATE OF ACCEPTANCE (Life is still a mess and you won't let go.)
WORRY (All worry is unnecessary.)
LACK OF HONESTY WITH YOURSELF (Ignoring messages because you   don't want to confront yourself.)

These suggestions are only the beginning of the transformation required in you. Perhaps you can view this as a mini-lesson in enlightenment. There are two sets of metaphysical searchers: Those who study metaphysics to figure out how to deal with the voluminous ground-level problems they have created in this lifetime, and those who have let go and are pursuing a more spiritually-oriented eternal journey. It is much simpler to astral project if you are of the second group. The reason for that is simple. If you are constantly worrying about problems in your life, or your drama, then there is little room left in your mind to focus on matters of more spiritual content. There are also some personal issues that can prevent you from growth if they are not dealt with. . .like releasing your past, and behavior that no longer suits the path you seek.

MARTYR-HOOD

Martyr-hood is so common in present society because of

the ever-prevalent belief which tells you that the only way you will make it to heaven is if you help others *at the expense* of yourself. Everyone has tales to tell of selfless giving to others. And, not so surprisingly, many people get a lot of ego-fulfillment from martyr-hood, simply because everyone views it as the ultimate in self-giving.

Martyr-hood is manipulation, and most martyrs engage in doing things for others that they are not asked to do, and then expect to be appreciated for it. They use guilt to make the victims of their abuse feel as though they should feel more obligated to the poor victimized martyr whom no one loves or understands enough.

Martyr-hood helps only those who engage in it. It makes them feel worthy of love from God. But, in reality, it is a cowardly act committed to prevent the individual from taking responsibility for their own well-being.

If you are being victimized by a martyr, release them with love.

RELEASING WITH LOVE

Remember that anyone who has control over you is simply doing what you have allowed them to do. The answer, though, is to release them with love.

Consciously decide that you will no longer tolerate any behavior that does not befit a part of God. As part of God you deserve to be treated with love and respect, not intolerance and manipulation. Realize that these type of people are sucking your energy, and you are allowing it. Disallow it. When an abhorrent or intolerable behavior surfaces towards you, you simply state, "I love you but, I will not tolerate _____ or _____ from you. If you choose to display that behavior anyway, I will not allow you in my reality. Make good on your promises. If you have someone close to you who you simply cannot physically separate from, such as your child or another family member that lives with you, you need to accept their reality and separate your self from it.

Remember that everyone creates their own reality, and you cannot be responsible for another's illusion. You will not help them or yourself by taking responsibility for them. In fact, you inhibit their growth by allowing them to avoid their life issues.

ACCEPTING OTHERS' REALITIES

We all have people in our lives who refuse to make their lives better. They are bitter, unhappy and blame everyone in the world but themselves for their miserable state of mind. No matter how obvious their mistakes, they will not take responsibility for any of them. They are life's "victims." Accept the reality that they are not ready to grow. Distance yourself if you can.

Accept their reality as their own. Don't participate in it, accept blame for it, or try to change it. They will remain negative until they consciously choose to change. Don't offer pity, as that only fuels their martyr-hood. Accept that *they* are in charge.

Finally, put those people, and the world, in the hands of God. Trust that everyone is educable and will awaken in time. Trust that they, too, can see the light. But perhaps they are not ready yet. Know that they have guides to take care of them, and that whatever horrible reality they may create, they cannot truly be injured or hurt. They are eternal. They will be okay. God leaves no one behind.

DISPOSING OF YOUR EGO

Every life ever experienced has been a drama worth writing a book about. So, why is it so important that your drama be better or worse than the rest of the world's? Why must you have the worst life in history? Or the most significant accomplishments? Why is it so hard for you to be happy for someone who has had success? Why can't you truly feel good about another's talents? Why do you still feel sorry for those who live wretched lives? There is a difference between empathy and sympathy. Why is it so scary to let go of your story and become one with God? Is it because you feel your "drama" defines you. Sorry, you are a part of God, and this drama is but a tiny, tiny part of you. Is it really so terrifying to realize that the you-ness that you experience here in the physical realm is not who you really are?

We are all sparks of God, that is who you really are. Is it really so difficult to let go of your story, and become one with all that is? When you do astral project, will you again feel superior to those who do not? Will you again think you are more special, or will you be able to humble yourself to your guides and teachers and really confront yourself? Will you realize that you have just begun and have many miles to go to full understanding? Can you truly feel gratitude, or will that threaten your ego? And, finally, are you truly willing to let that ego go?

If you don't let go of your ego, chances are you will never experience significant astral travel. Let it go, and grow!

Choose to begin living in positive energy. It really is your choice. No matter what happens, there is always a positive side to it. Ask yourself, "What did I want to learn from this?" rather than, "Why did God do this to me?" If you worry a lot about improving other people, focus that energy on the one person you can have an effect on, yourself!

HAVE FUN! Do not take your spiritual journey so seriously all the time. Enjoy life, as that is what spirituality is all about. Laughter is the essence of spirituality. Do not shroud yourself in solemnity.

Take full responsibility for your reality and its creation. Perhaps, you can also take it more lightly. Just because you create a hardship, does not mean there is a need to get down on yourself. All hardships teach. Stop feeling sorry for yourself and find the lesson. That way you won't do it again. Everything is your choice.

Ask yourself these three questions: Am I happy? Do I love? Am I positive? If you answered yes, you have done what you came here to do.

The most important thing for you to learn in your physical lifetimes is unconditional acceptance and love! ALLOW yourself to really feel the vastness of love and you will. If you truly desire to know what it is to feel that God- love, you can. This is the sole reason we are here, to learn to love despite our limited manifestations. That is your goal.

One of the hardest things to do is to look at yourself and accept your twin nature, your good and bad qualities. We all have that twin nature in our physical form. Forgive yourself and move on.

Remember, laughter is the essence of spirituality. Indulge in it often.

When I astral project, I remember it consciously. This

means that I will remember an astral experience in the same way that I remember my daily life. If I speak with a guide out of my body, it will be essentially the same as a conversation I might have with my husband, other than the content. My body is asleep, but my conscious mind is completely alert and aware. I **experience** my astral experiences to the fullest, as I experience my daily life in the physical realm. You can too.

CHAPTER THREE
MECHANICS

There are a few things that would be helpful for you to know before you experience astral travel. These are what they are.

VIBRATIONAL STATE

You enter into the vibrational state before leaving the body. Remember, however, to allow yourself to experience it in whatever way it comes. Your experiences may differ from mine.

Once it begins, your body will feel like it is shaking uncontrollably to a rhythmic hum. Your physical body will not move, however, as it is the frequency of your etheric body causing this sensation. That frequency is much higher than your physical body frequency. You may have experienced this before and been frightened by it, as it is a very powerful sensation; thus, there will be no doubt in your mind that this is what is occurring when it happens.

You may also hear sounds similar to jet engine noises, freight train sounds, or voices talking. Whichever way you experience it, those are the sounds of the astral plane. It may seem loud, as the vibrational rate of everything on the astral plane is so much higher than the physical.

You can compare the feeling you get with that of a scuba diver upon returning to the surface of the ocean. The difference in pressure can be compared to the difference in frequency. After a few times, however, it will feel very natural.

LIFTING OUT

You can get out of your body in a number of ways.

You may try rolling out. Simply act as if you are going to roll over, and you will roll out of your physical shell.

Willing yourself out is the method I currently use. It did take some time, however, for me to master this technique. It is as it sounds: you think yourself out. Some of you may find this very simple and natural.

Another method you might try is to ask your guides to lift you out. Sometimes they will do this, especially in the beginning to make you feel secure.

If none of these work for you, try whatever works for you.

THE GOD-MIND CONNECTION

Once you get into the vibrational state, you will feel a definite connection to the God mind or all that is. The intensity of that connection will grow when you explore higher dimensions of reality.

As we are all parts of God, we are all connected to him. The physical illusion, however, blocks us from feeling that connection, thus separateness. You will feel the oneness of all beings, and, most importantly, an overwhelming sense of peace, joy, and love. It is the ultimate high.

Knowledge of the divine plan, and of your own spiritual growth will be available to you. In this state you understand, you no longer feel separate, you are in ecstasy, overflowing with love.

The purpose of your physical illusion, the game we play, becomes known. Material gain is no longer important, spiritual gain is. Feeling the incredible strength of the energy source called love, you will know that love is all that is, it powers the universe.

Someone once said to me that, to him, it felt like he could feel all of humankind taking a breath, all at the same time. I did not feel it that way, but it certainly is a beautiful description of how one person felt it!

SIGHT, SOUND AND MOVEMENT

All your senses are controlled by your mind, your thoughts. If you can accept that, you will do fine.

One thing to avoid doing, is to compare your astral capabilities with your physical. Your sight may be different, or sounds may be heard differently. The important thing is to let yourself experience it in whatever way it is. Vision is different on different planes of existence. For example, the astral plane has a twilight type of look, the creative realms appear white to me. Some realms look like colored sparklers, and the earth plane usually looks about the same as when I am in my physical body. All of your senses will come from your entire being or consciousness, not from a physically-designated area.

Sometimes, voices or thoughts on the astral plane may have a "megaphone" quality to them. When you get closer to the light, or experience light beings, the vibrational buzzing sounds may increase. Another phenomena in the astral plane are crowd noises in what appear to be empty spaces. These are the thoughts of earth and astral beings, and they can consist of both words and music.

With astral movement you must consider movement of the whole, rather than movement of the parts. Wading or swimming movements may result in a small amount of movement, but the mind holds the true key to major travel out of the body. If you still harbor the physical barriers in terms of what you can and cannot do, you may need to confront those. If you cannot believe in your ability to fly, you will block your natural instincts from taking over. Remember, you have flown for thousands of years, you've just forgotten how. Flying is a great recreational activity! Fly the friendly skies!

CREATING REALITY

Thoughts are things. We know this to be true in our physical reality, as well as the astral. On the astral plane, however, where your thoughts appear before your eyes, this reality must be faced head on. If you think of something, it will appear before your eyes. If you think of someone, you will either go to them, or a holographic image will appear. A little hint that might help you on your travels is something that I learned somewhat further down the road. When confronted with a person you know, notice whether or not there are feelings towards them. Note how they respond. Do they respond as they would normally, or are they responding to your thoughts? This is how you tell the difference between an entity and a thought-form of an entity. The one that displays feelings, and responds in the normal response pattern for that being is the real entity. Thought-form entities will respond exactly how you want them to respond, whether it be in fear or in love. They will reflect your **true** desire, not necessarily your conscious desire.

Another reason the creation of reality is extremely important is the exposure that many of you may have to beliefs in negative entities. Let me make it as clear as I can that they do not exist, and if you run into a demon or burning fires or lakes, it is only your unconscious or conscious fear that you are responding to. All you need to do is confront the "entity" or the "hell" and it will disappear. You **must** confront your fear or you will never go past it.

Some tell you to surround yourself in white light. If it makes you feel good, then do it. But, remember that you *are* white light. You are a part of God, for heaven's sakes. If God is with you, then who can be against you? Ask your guides to only expose you to beings who are of the light, until you feel more secure. That way, you will not need to deal with lost souls or astral work, until you are ready.

That astral work can be quite varied. One of my purposes is to work with lost souls, which I will get into more later. There are astral support groups and subconscious work. Subconscious work is making spiritual contact with people on the earth who are not ready to remember such things consciously, but their subconscious is working very hard at accepting new things, so that the conscious mind can catch up. This means you may visit some people you know, and they will have no conscious memory of it. Subconscious contact is important and productive. Do not doubt the validity of what you are doing simply because of the lack of conscious recall.

TELEPATHY AND SENSING REALITIES

Communication with entities in other dimensions is telepathic, and you will hear all the thoughts of the earth-plane beings. Sometimes it may sound like echoes, as you hear the thought directly before it is spoken.

Upon observation of an entity or individual, you may be provided with information on their past, present, or future. I call this sensing realities. There is no need to validate your information, as so many feel compelled to do, by finding physical documentation. The God-mind is a higher authority. Trust it.

Much information will come to you in the astral body, that physically you would not sense. A great teacher is with you: listen. Trust your instincts. You are a spiritual being, and your light shines. Trust yourself.

Experiences of materialization are possible, which usually occur only for spiritual purposes; the light, which, when immersed in its glow you will feel only peace; past life experiences, which can become quite elaborate and exciting, and much more. Do not limit yourself. Changes may occur in your physical life as you may begin to channel, your intuitive senses may increase, spiritual presences become more pronounced, dreams become more conscious and powerful, and you may tune into other dimensions. If for any reason anything you experience makes you uncomfortable, simply choose not to experience it.

One thing to keep in mind is that the state of consciousness one needs to reach before entering the vibrational state is pretty deep. Many books, probably including mine, make it sound as if you just close your eyes and fly away. Perhaps there are some people who can do that, but I tend to feel that most people will be like me. It may take a half-hour to an hour to reach the deep level of consciousness for the vibrational state to begin. Someone asked me once if they could go astral in meditation. When your consciousness leaves the body, the body is in a very deep state of sleep, but your conscious mind is awake. In order for me to leave my body, my physical shell has to reach a very deep level of relaxation and then sleep. It takes me at least thirty minutes, sometimes longer to reach that state. I have never gone astral during meditation; however, I have fallen asleep during meditation and then gone astral. Be patient with yourself.

The bottom line is that this is entirely up to you. You choose whether or not you are going to implement these new ideas and techniques into your everyday life, and you will decide whether to let go of the past, and experience the future. YOU ARE IN CHARGE!

If you have doubts about the existence of astral projection, ask yourself a few questions. How can you prove a multi-dimensional reality with three-dimensional standards? How can you prove a non-physical reality with physical standards? How can you honestly say that you believe in life after death, but then dispute every contact with that life? I know the reality of what I have experienced. The only way you can know for sure is to do it yourself.

The next chapter deals with higher vibrations. As I enter into a new phase of my growth, I begin to understand just how ignorant I am. I experience a humbling effect in witnessing the reality of God, and the totality of unconditional love. Come with me, as I experience the adventure of a lifetime!

CHAPTER FOUR
HIGHER VIBRATIONS

THE LOST SOUL

After driving home from a trip to a neighboring city, I went to bed. It was summertime and we had air conditioning. Despite the comfortable temperature of our home, I began to sweat and feel extremely ill-at-ease. Ignoring it, I went to sleep. My husband rolled over and mumbled something about the heat, and went back to sleep.

After falling into a deep dream-state, I began dreaming a very violent and frightening dream. In the dream, I and Andy, my husband, were driving down the highway, when suddenly a frantic man began to run in front of our vehicle. Visual thought-forms, images of his confused and terrified thoughts, surrounded his being. This man was extremely angry, frustrated and confused.

Trying to remain calm, we drove past the man, immediately assuming he was a lunatic. But, as soon as we passed him, we came upon a very terrible accident. Several people lay dead in the street, their bodies mangled. Andy and I passed through the sight feeling very sick, hoping to erase the memory of the horror we witnessed. Within seconds, we were surrounded by police cars, blocking off the highway. No one would be allowed through until the accident was cleaned up.

Waking up in a very cold sweat, I was absolutely terrified. Feeling a little angry at my guides for allowing me to experience such negativity, I told them I would not allow this into my reality, whatever it may be. And, furthermore, they should know better than to scare me like that! The joke was on me, as I experienced the dream over and over until, after the third time, I realized I had to confront it.

Still extremely scared, I asked my guides to please help me understand what was happening. What could this be, and why was I creating such a fearful reality? My guides quickly intervened.

When returning from the neighboring city, we had picked up a hitchhiker, so to speak...a man who had died in the car accident, and had since become lost, sensed my openness and tagged along. His guides led him to me to help him move on.

Many people who die quick and violent deaths don't realize they have passed on. After all, they don't feel any different. Sometimes, people who had no knowledge of spirituality, God, or didn't believe in life after death while they were physical, find themselves in a precarious situation when they die. They may not even have the ability to recognize spiritual beings, thus, they don't see their guides. Their reality is so grounded in physicality, that they wander about the earth trying to get their loved ones attention. When the people they love don't even recognize that they are there, or that they exist, the lost souls panic. The soul has suffered a very traumatic death, and now, the soul is caught in a void of space all alone, or so it seems. I have even run into souls who believe very strongly that they are going to be sent to hell, and so, despite their ability to see the light and move on, they wait. They will wait until somebody comes and takes them to hell. This is why thousands of physical beings like myself volunteer before coming into the physical realm to be a physical vantage point for the lost soul. Their guides enlist our help, and we simply lead them to their guides and the light.

There are five things of importance in the lost souls mind: recognition, love, respect, understanding, and empowerment. Recognizing that they are there, is a great relief to the lost soul, who has been trying to talk to someone in a physical body for days or weeks. Love, respect, and understanding are also important, and if you allow yourself to feel the confusion the being is feeling, the compassion and understanding will flow naturally. When an entity shows you a thought-form of his frightening death, tell him you understand that he has suffered, and you feel for him. Let him know that he is loved and that you will help him. The last thing you will do with the confused being is empower him with knowledge. All he needs to know is that he will not be judged and that his spirit guides are waiting to embrace him and welcome him back to the spirit realm. Tell him to follow the light, and let him know that he is greatly loved by God. Give the entity the option of staying with you for a few hours or days, until he feels comfortable enough to take the next step. Usually, they leave within thirty minutes. The reason for this is that it is frightening for them to leave the only physical contact they have had. Once they search their spirit and recognize the truth of what you are telling them, they will be ready.

The situation was not negative at all; my perception was an illusion. A fellow being was in need of assistance, and in this spirit's mind, he was still physically alive and at the accident scene trying to get help! I had been brought in to give him that help.

Communicating telepathically to the entity, I felt his incredible need to cling to me. This was natural, yet, uncomfortable for me. I affirmed to the entity my need for space, and he respected that. Remember, with lost souls, you also create your own reality, and they cannot do anything you don't allow. You cannot be "possessed," but you can feel uncomfortable in the presence of a lost soul, so do not allow them to permeate your being. Protect your space.

Having had no experience with this sort of thing, I handled it with less than precision. That is okay, as the important thing is that they found their way. And, if for some reason, you can not help the entity, fear not, for they will most certainly be led to someone else who can.

"I love you, but you must look behind you and see the light of God! Call out to your guides, ask them to take you there! You are no longer of the physical plane, you have moved onto greater things. Turn around, ask! His response was one of resistance, and the heat intensified. In my own inexperience and panic, I responded by ordering him to leave my presence. "In the name of Jesus Christ, I can no longer help you, turn and go to the light! A sudden gush of ecstasy could be felt as the entity saw the light, a cool breeze whizzed over my body as the entity soared towards the loving light of God. Another lost soul found home.

My mistake was a common one. In my fear I had felt threatened by the entity's presence. It was unloving of me to order him to leave, and there is no need to throw around Jesus's name to help a lost soul. As this was my first experience, I had a lot to learn, and over time, I would learn to master the art.

It is important to explain reality to the soul. As this is their first lesson in spirituality, it is very important to explain matter-of-factly what the light is, who your guides are, what they do, and other questions that the entity might have. Dealing with lost souls can be a very calm and peaceful experience, if you allow yourself to see from the spiritual reality rather than the physical illusion. Lost souls have no true desire to harm anyone, they need help. Sometimes, the only way they can get someone's attention is to do strange things, such as knocking things to the ground or other poltergeist-like activities. All they want, is your help. They are lost.

Never fear the spiritual realm. Your guides will never bring anything to you unless they are absolutely sure you can handle it. If something seems frightening, change your point of perception, as, there is absolutely nothing to fear in the universe. Fear is illusion. Anything that does not reflect love is an illusion! You are the light, and part of God. You are capable of everything. All there is, is love!

LEAPS OF LIGHT

After leaving my body, I was whisked to a beautiful dimension. A black space, and the thought-forms in this dimension manifested in a yellow light. Musical chambers echoing the most beautiful celestial music I had ever heard, surrounded me. These chambers were like rectangular lights with no definite edges, as they were rounded, and the music that emanated from them touched the very core of your being.

Entities of all sorts were there, astral travelers, those who had passed on, and my own spiritual guides who waited for me, beaming with happiness.

I lay down on a board made of yellow light, and waited for whatever was to come. One of my guides lifted his arm, and the musical chambers began to emanate even more energy from their core, bringing my spirit into a state of energy overload. Feeling peaceful and comfortable, the vibrational frequency of my body continued to increase. When the energy got over-powering, my guides transmuted it into my being, a skill I would later learn to do myself. The feeling of vibrational bliss cannot be explained, as I was an engine, being fine-tuned and brought up to maximum capacity. Little did I know that with your consciousness, there is no such thing as maximum capacity, as it will continue to grow and grow through eternity.

The other beings were very happy as I went through the process, in fact, they were having a party in celebration. The joy and elation I felt were indescribable, and so immense.

I returned to my body feeling like a new person.

This was the first in what turned out to be many vibrational raisings. The purpose of this type of experience is to bring you up to a management level, a level more suitable to astral projection and traveling in higher dimensions.

Sensitivity of the spiritual realm becomes more prevalent when you are in your body. Once you begin to travel the realms, your guides will do this often, as you will have a need for higher and higher vibrations to reach higher teachers.

A VIBRATIONAL HEALING

Having returned to the same realm mentioned previously, my being lay in mid-air as six entities, some of whom were my guides, stood around me, three on each side.

Observing the colors and vibrational patterns of my being, they determined what medical problems I was experiencing and the reason for the manifestation. I understood the reasons for the manifestation of an ovarian cyst. My husband wanted another child and we were trying to have one, but deep down inside, I was not ready for another child. Perhaps I would never be ready for another one. Our child had been extremely difficult since her birth, and I could not deal with another child and still be happy. The entities raised their hands as beams of white light shone down from them, healing my auric disturbance causing the cyst. Immense warmth was felt, as the healing ensued.

When they were finished, one of my guides explained that my other problem, which was later diagnosed as asthma, could not be healed yet, as I did not understand the reasons for the manifestation. Some soul-searching would be in order.

I returned to my body and, as expected, my cyst had disappeared.

A CATHEDRAL CALLING

After leaving my body, I was taken to a beautiful cathedral

filled with Sunday worshippers. The ceiling was rounded and painted beautifully, and stained glass windows decorated the walls of the huge building.

Feeling very joyful, I flew about the cathedral spreading love energy throughout. Facial expressions didn't change, but almost the entire congregation felt my presence subconsciously, telepathically asking questions, "What does it feel like to do that?" I responded with descriptions of what I was doing. "I just went through the ceiling, now I'm floating to the floor, now through it. Out the window I go, oops! I'm coming back!" Receiving affirmations from their subconscious minds, meaning a telepathic communication with that part of their mind, I went back to my body.

This is one example of many types of work done on the spiritual plane, as there are hundreds of methods that the other side employs in helping those of us in the physical realm. Some of those exciting things will be explored further along in my journey.

A LESSON IN REALITIES

While visiting a friend of mine in her home, I began to sense a very obvious presence. Heat sensations, as well as a very strong pressure traveled through my body. The feelings were so strong, and I responded to them so heavily, that I assumed, incorrectly, that I was dealing with a very distraught lost soul.

My friend, who ironically shares my name (Marilyn), noticed immediately that something was bothering me, and explained to her my sensations and my first conclusion. She said that she had been feeling a heat around her home for about two weeks, and was quite intrigued that I felt the same and more.

We went to the basement and got into a comfortable position to communicate with the entity. My impression was that the entity was very negative because of my strong reaction to his presence. My cheeks twitched, my back was flinching, and my head began to pound in pain, and an unexplainable anger crept up on me, and my friend was a bit surprised. No matter how I looked at it, I did not feel empathy for this "lost soul."

I asked my guides to help me to understand the situation, and some information came through, but it was vague. The entity communicated a desire for forgiveness from his wife and child, as he was concerned that they would never forgive him. My response was that, of course they would forgive him, we all have to die! But, he persisted, and the more he continued, the angrier I felt.

In my ignorance of the whole story, I explained the light to the entity, going into detail about his guides and all of that. Getting angrier, I felt a need to be more forceful as his energy was interfering with me too much physically. I was beginning to feel very sick, but all I could get from him, was the need for forgiveness from his wife and child.

After a short period of time, I yelled at the entity, telling him he had to leave, as his energy was interfering with mine too much. A cool breeze blew over, and I assumed he had left my presence. Not so, as I would learn later. He would return, as he had some unfinished business!

Returning from the meditative state, I was famished and my head was in so much pain. I could not understand how that could have happened. My initial feeling was that I had simply allowed the entity to permeate my being, thus, the physical discomfort. I vowed to never allow a lost soul to permeate my being again. You don't have to allow yourself to feel that much of what an entity is feeling. Later, I would understand why it had occurred.

Marilyn came to my house the next day, as she felt a strong need to read to me from a book that speaks in depth on issues of lost souls. She was feeling this entity again, but didn't let on.

Not long after she came into the house, I began to feel the presence again. The spirit seemed more peaceful, and I felt I had a better handle on protecting my own space. My friend read from the book, and we discussed some of the issues of being a lost soul, what it must feel like, the difficulty in leaving those you love behind, and the spirit seemed to soak it up. The encounter carried with it none of the previous negativity, and I felt that the spirit might be reconciling with the woman and child. A distinct chill ran through my body, and the spirit left. At the time, we assumed he had gone to the light, another lost soul finding home. We were wrong.

My friend visited a very spiritual woman by the name of Theresia. This woman is known for her work drawing charcoal pictures of your guides and your past lives. She is extremely aware, and picked up on the entity right away.

Theresia explained that the entity was a very powerful, protective, Indian spirit. As Marilyn's protective spirit, he had a strong desire to be acknowledged and to communicate with her. Theresia told Marilyn to ask me how I felt about Indians.

At my home, Marilyn and I discussed Theresia's insights. From the moment she had entered my home I had felt the Indian spirit, but suddenly another feeling was coming. A duality was going on that I could not explain. *Remembering a lot of little things in my past denoting a fascination with Indians, I began to feel a clearer message.*

Emotions began to run rampant again, not anger, but love.

The spirit began communication again, and I realized that I was the woman from whom he sought forgiveness. Perhaps we were married in another lifetime, and he had died, leaving me alone with a child. My response to his presence was due to my own feelings, not his. Feeling like a schoolgirl falling in love, I allowed myself to remember the feelings of that lifetime. There was still confusion, however, as I could not understand why this Indian would be my friend's protective spirit when there was such a strong connection to me.

We began to acknowledge the spirit's presence verbally and asked him to respond. A strap to our high chair began to slowly sway back and forth, and I knew I had understood something right this time, but there had to be more.

The next morning the Indian came to visit me, and in tears, I forgave him. This felt rather odd, as I did not remember any details of this lifetime, only the emotions I had felt. Suddenly, I knew why this Indian chose to return at this time. Since my marriage to my husband, I had been obsessed with becoming a widow. The Indian was warning me that I could create that reality. My obsession with my husband's possible death could be the creator of it. What a loving gesture, I thought, to return and teach me this lesson. It was not over, though, as the Indian returned several times and showered me with love feelings. This is hard to describe, it can only be described as a non-physical hug. Out of nowhere, you feel overcome with love and emotion. I knew there was more to the story, and consulted Theresia. She did not know that I had figured out the connection between me and the Indian. I asked her to draw my guides and past-lives, and what she came up with was amazing.

The duality I felt became clear when Theresia explained that there were actually two Indians, my friend, Marilyn's Indian, and the Indian who was involved in my past life. Apparently, in Indian custom, when a man hurts a woman emotionally, he is expected to have a male intermediary approach her for forgiveness, and this is what was happening with us. But the life we shared together was quite different than I had expected.

My present-life husband, Andy, and I were married to each other, both white, and living on a western fort. Andy was a cavalry officer during the Indian wars, thus, gone a lot.

Feeling an attraction to the Indians and their way of life, and seeing how they were treated, I began to bring them food and become friends with them. Eventually, it turned into an escape operation. Whenever suspicion arose regarding the lengthy amount of time I would spend with the Indians, I would use the excuse of teaching them about Christianity.

An especially wanted Indian was taken prisoner, wanted because of his expertise in battle planning against the cavalry. We spent time together, and eventually, we fell in love. We had a very deep spiritual love for each other that differed from what I and Andy had in that lifetime.

The time came when it was the Indian's turn to escape. I had the choice to go with him, but declined, as I loved my husband and wanted to make it work. The Indians were living through hard times, and I wasn't sure I could handle such a drastic change in lifestyle.

Not long after his departure, it became clear that I was pregnant, and rumors spread that it was not my husband's child, as he was not at the fort at the time of conception. When I had the child, obviously Indian, everyone knew that not only did I have an affair with an Indian, which was considered a social stigma, but I was the one who was letting prisoners escape!

My husband left me, and soon after, died on the battlefield. His anger was more at the fact that I had an affair with an **Indian,** than the affair itself, as that disgraced him.

Suffering a lot of ridicule and scorn from the fort community, I became bitter over time. Wonder over whether the Indian really loved me, or if he had just used me, began entering my mind, and, before long, I felt totally abandoned and unloved. Manifesting tuberculosis, I died a few years later, leaving my child with my sister to raise.

The irony of the whole story was that *the Indian* loved me very much and, regardless of the danger, would have returned to take me with him, if he had but known of my suffering. He never knew of our child until the day he died. Our separate cultures prevented us from fully understanding each other.

As you have probably deduced, my original reaction to the entity was as a result of my subconscious memory. The Indian spirit near me rekindled my anger at the Indian who I perceived as having abandoned me.

Apparently, my Indian was very sad, as he had been trying to make contact with me for quite a while. He loved me very much, and he wanted to help me. What a guy! She didn't know the Indian's name, but a short while later, I learned his name was Red Jacket.

Theresia also picked up on another entity that would become very important to me. I would later learn his name to be Emmanuel. She drew him with purple and green around him, the color of the lights I saw in my meditative states. He was my spiritual teacher, and he was going to help me feel oneness!

She sensed several past lives. A life around the time of Jesus Christ, in which I had the opportunity to become a disciple of his, but chose not to because of the way it would look. (Not a good decision!) A Manchurian wizard, where I came so close to becoming a master, but did not because of my lackadaisical attitude; a Greek lifetime where I died during the Turkish invasion; a journalist/publisher lifetime, where I had great respect from the townsfolk, but treated my family like dog meat. All those lifetimes were male lifetimes, which Theresia felt I enjoyed more than my female lives, because I did not enjoy the oppressive lifestyles of women, and I would tend to get hurt more in my female lifetimes. She sensed that in one other female lifetime, I was a nun in France with my older sister who was Mother Superior. That sister was my friend Marilyn in this lifetime. An interesting thing occurred when showing these pictures to Andy, as his immediate response was that of anger, his subconscious memory rekindled. His response was, "It's bad enough that you messed around on me, but did it have to be with an Indian?!" Quite confirming commentary, wouldn't you say?

This particular love triangle would turn out to be a major part of my lessons on oneness. My whole perception of love was being challenged, as well as my husband's. Love is inclusive, rather than exclusive. Red Jacket and I had a very spiritual love: how could that be wrong? The mistake was in taking it to the point of physical expression. The love, however, was right. Love is too vast to be compartmentalized into possessive boxes. Love expands, it does not contract. When you love one person, you cannot help but become more loving towards others, as that love for the individual grows into love for mankind. My understanding of love was so minute at that point, but it was destined to grow and grow!

TEPEE

After expressing my desire to meet my Indian on the astral plane, as I wanted to understand why I had made some of the choices I had, we met. One major question on my mind was why I did not leave with the Indian. After all, I apparently loved him very much.

Red Jacket took me to an old Indian camp, sparsely populated and very dirty. Several tepees were scattered about with a fire pit in the middle of the camp. The people were very poor, as little food was available and they scavenged for whatever they could get. Autumn winds were just blowing in, and it was apparent that winter was on its way. How many of these poor souls would even survive the winter, I wondered.

Most of the people in the camp were Indian women, as the men were off to battle. A few children who had survived the wretched conditions played in the dirt. No happiness could be seen in the Indian faces, just suffering.

The answer was obvious that Red Jacket could not leave his people in these conditions, and I could not bring myself to join them, thus giving up my fairly comfortable lifestyle.

In this experience, I did not speak with my Indian, but his presence was very clearly guiding me on my way. More direct contact would be forthcoming, along with deeper understandings of that lifetime, and what it meant.

A strong desire existed within me to reunite with this man. It is difficult to explain the feelings of love you have for a being no longer in physical form, but those feelings were very strong. I was able to fully access the emotions of that lifetime, and I knew that we had loved each other a great deal.

More and more contact was being made in subtle ways with the teacher I would eventually come to know as Emmanuel. His thoughts and mine were mingling quite a bit, and his input was becoming a regular part of my existence. Oneness was his area of expertise, and small pieces of understanding were beginning to arise. If I would look at someone in a store with distaste, I would hear his voice in my head, "We are all one, that being you look down upon is part of you." Feeling ashamed, I would try to look at others in a new non-judgmental way, though I would not always accomplish this as, inevitably, sometimes my ego interferes. It is interesting to me that sometimes people believe that because I am involved in so much astral travel, that somehow, I should be more perfect than others. This is in no way true, as when I return to my physical body, I am stuck with all my physical limitations, including the ego, and I make mistakes.

Oneness cannot be explained, as it is a feeling, but one scenario describes it well. The tiny molecules in our bodies can accomplish very little on their own, but when they come together they form a human being whose functions flow perfectly, as one. Similarly, each consciousness on it's own may have little impact in the workings of the universe, but as one consciousness we flow to the energy force of love and the divine plan is implemented with ease. An example of that oneness is my own writing. As a writer, I am nothing without the people who build word processors, because without them, I have no tools to write with. Most fields of expertise require tools that they do not create. This is a visual and very physically-oriented description of oneness, and oneness is a feeling. A feeling that every being is a part of you, and a state of unconditional acceptance.

JOURNEY INWARD

Entering into the vibrational state, I began to will myself out of body. The voice of my teacher could be heard telling me it was not necessary to leave my body in order to travel amongst the dimensions.

Forcing myself to go inward, I entered into a new reality. I was not using my visual capabilities, but sensed that I was no longer in tho same space I previously occupied. My teacher spoke with me and I expressed great interest in the rate of speed that my mind seemed to be working. Inherently, I knew that I was feeling what it was like to be dead, and I was surprised at the tremendous mind activity still going on. Consensus reality looks upon death as a horrible ending, when in reality, it is a wonderful beginning! In this state of connected-ness with the God-mind, I fully understood one-ness, as there is an awesome connection to all that is when you leave the confines of your physical illusion. As we choose to enter physical bodies to experience that limitedness, that separation from God, that illusion disappears once you exit that manifestation. The lesson in astral projection is to some-how bring that feeling back into your limited form and ex-perience and share it in this physical reality. Words cannot describe that feeling, as it is total, unconditional love.

I returned to my body and awoke.

A day later, entering into the vibrational state again, I left my body and wandered about the house. The vibrations were extremely strong and my head literally felt like exploding from the tremendous energy emanating through my being. Returning to my body, I prepared to journey inward.

Going through an intense vibrational raising, I had an opportunity to speak with Red Jacket. When I returned to my body later, I only remembered that we conversed and could not remember what we said. My teacher wanted me to know there were still blocks for me to work out before I could experience a full conscious meeting.

After my meeting with Red Jacket was over, my teacher came in and continued the process of raising my vibrations. A feeling of such deep love could be felt whenever he was near, I could not help but feel the same for him.

Emmanuel taught me how to transmute the tremendous amounts of energy he was sending through my being by taking the energy, and bringing it to a level of love. I stopped fighting the energy and allowed it into my being, thus, flow-ing with the energy, rather than against it. At some moments, my head felt like exploding, but upon transmutation, the energy expanded into love and my being exploded in light!

After about an hour, I begged my teacher to stop, as I could not handle any more energy! I awoke moments later, feeling the residual hum of my tuned-up spirit, a buzzing sensation throughout my body for hours afterwards. Electrified, my awareness had changed. What an exciting journey!

Learning to operate in a higher level of vibration is an essential aspect of astral travel, as reaching higher dimensions requires a brighter light. If you enter into a dimension too high for your being, you will be overwhelmed by the power. You can't be hurt in any way, but you may feel as though the energy could crush you. This is why these vibrational raisings are so important. They are your key to further enlightenment and understanding.

CHAPTER FIVE
REPORTING ON THE STARS

My professional background before assuming the role of mother and homemaker, was general assignment reporting. Some of the experiences I began to have, seemed to be geared for that background, as the universe was my beat, and my spirit was the camera.

THE DISASTER TEAM

After expressing an interest to my teacher about what those on the other side do at the scene of big disasters where many people die, I was sent to cover the disaster team.

Suiting up in silver boots and a silver helmet, I joined a group of spirits who helped victims of airplane disasters, earthquakes, tornadoes, bad car accidents, fires, and all types of traumatic, sudden-death situations. Everyone in the crew manifested the boots and helmets for the sake of the souls crossing over, as in the confusion of fires and wreckage, the physical familiarity was key. Manifesting in a physical way captured the attention of dying souls, who were in shock.

The disaster crew works non-stop, as they are whisked from one disaster to another all over the globe. They feel it when they are needed, and quickly will themselves to the sight. Their job is to pull the dying souls out of the mess, and hand them over to their spiritual guides, as there is always a lot of wreckage, smoke, and physical obstruction. The souls who have died are usually quite disoriented, and they do not realize they have passed on. Regardless, they can't seem to see past the wreckage to where they need to go.

We handled about fifteen disasters on the night I worked with them, as they are constantly going from one location to another. After a couple of hours of work I went onto my next assignment. . .

ASTRAL SUPPORT GROUPS

After my encounter with the disaster crew, I needed a little time to wind down. I was taken to several groups of entities, who all appeared to be subconscious astral, meaning that they were not consciously aware of this visit, and were probably sleeping.

Each group had a different twist, but all dealt with an aspect of spirituality. We all go to these types of groups at night, and seldom remember them. This is one way that subconscious work is accomplished with those of us in our physical illusion. Love, support, and growth were the goals of these groups.

The group I spent the most time with was a group that enjoyed playing a game called negative/positive. As this was something I was working on at that point in my life, it was helpful to me. The object of the game was to find the positive angle to every negativity thrown your way. The group leader, who appeared to be a spiritual guide, would say something negative, and our goal was to find the positive angle. We played the game for several rounds, and everyone, including myself, was excited about the positive transference that was possible with negative situations.

We all go to groups that cover aspects of our own spiritual growth in our sleep. Whatever you may be going through, there is a group that covers it! Many who have just passed over go to these groups in their transition back to the spiritual world. It certainly isn't boring on the other side. The word death is such a misrepresentation.

THE ROBBER'S TALE

During the night, a recurring dream about the death of a robber began.

A couple had taken a walk in their neighborhood, leaving a fairly young child alone in the house. While they were gone, a robber had entered the house, and finding the child, locked her in the closet.

Upon returning from their walk, the couple noticed the broken glass and found their little girl. Police cars were just arriving, as the neighbors had noticed a disturbance and called them. They went throughout the house to make sure the robber wasn't hiding, and came up with nothing. But they had not checked a room that was partially closed off, and the father asked them to check, just to be sure. Upon entering the room, the police were confronted with the robber and immediately fired five shots. The robber was dead, and now he was a lost soul.

Immediately, I began communication with the entity. Compassion for this entity over-flowed. Despite his obviously criminal status, it was his first major crime, and he had already made a decision that it would be his last. When he saw the little girl looking so frightened, it touched a part of him and he knew he had to change his ways. But his reality did not allow that, and now he felt that there was nothing left for him but to burn in hell! Amazingly, he had seen the light, but felt he must wait to be taken to hell.

The feelings were welling up in me for this entity, as I explained that God loved him. His intensity increased, causing a bit of physical discomfort, and asking him to please respect my space, he calmly complied. Explaining some universal truths and realities to him, he excitedly absorbed them. Reaffirming that he was greatly loved, I finished telling him what he needed to do and told him he could stay near me until he felt secure in leaving. His appreciation was clear, and a short time later, he turned, leaving a cool breeze in his wake.

ASTRAL PLANE SUICIDE

Journeying inward and into another dimension, I ran across another being's reality. The being had created thought-form tables and wasn't allowing people to pass by his tables without "proper" identification.

Confusion ran rampant inside of me, as I was viewing this situation from a physical perspective. Wanting to pass by, I created my own thought-form I.D., but he would not let me pass, saying I did not have the proper I.D. Creating many thought-form identification cards, including ones that I knew my husband had, he continually refused my passage.

Looking around, I noticed that several entities were fully aware of what was happening to me, but did not come to my aid.

Confused, I gave up and began pondering this reality in a corner of space, when a beautiful female entity appeared before me. She was a very wispy yellowish-white light being with flowing hair and dress. She explained to me that this man felt very unloved, as his wife had left him, he had no children, and he felt his family did not care; thus, he had committed suicide. Since then, creating this reality allowed him to reject other beings, the way he had felt rejected. When I arrived, he could sense that I had much love in my life, and this made him want to reject me.

As I had attempted suicide in this lifetime for similar reasons, I understood, and though the conclusion was an illusion, the pain was real. Returning to where he was, I hugged him and sent him thought-forms of my love and understanding. It was okay that he had treated me harshly, I understood. "I'm so sorry that you suffered so much in your lifetime, but you know, you really are loved greatly. Let go of this illusory reality you have created for yourself. There is so much more to be experienced. The universe is a loving place and you are an important part of us all." A moment of love was shared between us, and he began to release himself.

Apologizing for treating me like he did, the anger began to release from his being as he felt forgiveness for his wife and family. After a few moments of oneness with each other, as fellow beings of the same light, his reality disappeared, and he joined the other entities to move on towards the light.

A valuable lesson in oneness was learned. My original anger was replaced with understanding and love. Once I felt that, I was able to flow with the energy of the universe and help a fellow being in need. This can be applied to the physical realm, as we all know obnoxious people, but rarely try to understand the hurt that has created that behavior. We are all one, and we can feel that oneness with all life, if we so choose. Find out why, and do not judge.

OPENING CHANNELS

While visiting my friend Marilyn, my Indian's presence became very distinct, As we continued to chat, the energy was increasing, and I instinctively knew that he wanted to channel through me. I'd never channeled before, so I just went with the feeling and allowed the eternal to guide me.

Going into a meditative state, energy waves began to come through my body, beginning at my feet and up towards my head. When the connection was complete, I felt a jerking sensation in my head, by my sixth chakra (in between my eyes on my forehead) and my eyes jerked upwards.

Laughing hysterically, the Indian came through, and after ten minutes of uncontrollable laughter, Marilyn asked him what was so funny. He responded that it felt unusual to be in a body again, after all, it had been years since he had been in one. We found out that his name was Red Jacket. The name was connected to his status as a war planner in the Indian wars. My friend had been having a hard time selling her house, and he told her not to worry, it would sell. A few weeks later it did. He ended his chat by saying that he loved me very, very much, and that I had loved him very deeply, as well. Desiring to meet with me in the spiritual realm, he asked that I work towards that goal. Happy to have made it through, he bid his adieu.

ENERGY REFINEMENT

That night, an angelic being, displaying a very female essence, channeled into my being. Her goal was to instruct me on the channeling state, how to hold the energy more efficiently, and refining the energy to make a stronger connection. Working with me for about an hour, her essence was very loving and seemed very powerful. At the time, I believed this was going to help me channel Red Jacket. Time would prove the inaccuracy of my conclusion.

Later that day, Red Jacket channeled through me. Refining the energies, we did not speak. Perhaps it was necessary to complete this process a few times, before successful channeling contact could be made. This lasted a couple of hours, and it felt wonderful, rather like receiving a celestial hug. Afterwards, I felt closer to Red Jacket, as if some of my subconscious memories were being stirred up.

Theresia had said something about the Indians that became very clear to me. The Indians flowed with the divine plane of love, and, therefore, viewed death and separation differently than we. They were able to "hold" the love that they felt for someone in their hearts, rather than letting that love "hold" them down in grief or sorrow. Death or separation did not change what had come to pass. In their thoughts, they would think of the loved one in the context of the time they were

together, as if they were still there. Regardless of the circumstances of the separation, it did not change the love that
already existed. Red Jacket felt this way, and he wanted me to
feel that way, too. Still very involved in the physical illusion
of love, rather than the reality, there was much for me to learn.

VIETNAM

My daughter, Melissa, had been angry since the day she
was born, screaming for four months straight, and, after that,
she was frightened if anyone came to the house. The doctors
termed it hypertonism, but I knew there was more, so I
consulted Theresia.

Melissa was an American soldier with oriental blood who
fought and died in Vietnam. Traumatized by the war, in
particular, the innocent children being slaughtered, returning
to earth was especially frightening for her. She had wanted to
come back as a boy, but chose to become a girl so as to avoid
any possibility of repeating her previous war-torn life. She
saw the world as a scary place, understandably so.

Melissa, my husband and I, had other connections, too. In
my life with Red Jacket, she was my sister, and after my death,
she raised my Indian child. I was re-paying her by raising her
in this lifetime. We were sisters in many lifetimes, brothers in
others, and when we weren't related, we grew up together in
an orphanage. The interesting twist to the story was Andy's
involvement. My daughter and I were always in competition
for him. In one lifetime, Andy had courted both of us extensively, but decided to marry her because she was more traditional than I. It seems that in all my lifetimes, I have been more
on the racy side, Melissa more traditional. Andy and I had a
more passionate love for each other, but Melissa was traditional, and he knew she would take care of him. My feeling
was that he was small-minded to make such a decision, and I
was hurt. In our next lifetime, I had the affair. We were
balancing our karma. Interestingly, Melissa was a priest in the
same parish with me in my life as a nun. In fact, we had been
attracted to each other, but this made him (Melissa) feel very
uncomfortable, as it was too confrontational against the
church.

Melissa was here this time to learn to confront her reality,
and, to realize that life can be fun. She needed to break away

from doing what consensus reality expected from her, and instead, do what she felt was right.

It is interesting to see how many different types of relationships we have had with those we love. Clearly, love simply is. There is no distinction or categorizing of love in the spiritual realm, it just is.

EMMANUEL

Feeling a strong urgency to go into the channeling state, I had my husband set up a tape recorder and he prepared to be my partner. Andy was still a bit skeptical, but I felt I should give it a try, but as the entity began to come in, he ran to answer the ringing phone.

Surprised and excited, I learned that it was not Red Jacket who had come through, but my teacher, and his name was Emmanuel. Explaining that I needed to give Andy a little time, as he viewed my spiritual growth as a hobby, rather than a way of life, he asked me to be patient. Feeling a little angry at Andy, I did not accomplish this right away.

Emmanuel was an entity who was at the level that Christ was in his last incarnation. Jesus has evolved to be an even greater being.

It was important to Emmanuel that I learn to channel, as this would open up the doors of communication. His message was of oneness, and beingness, and it was important that I learn to "nest," as I had not done this in my other lifetimes. This was all information that Theresia had given me, and I asked Emmanuel about her. "She is an enlightened being who chose to return to earth to help in the physical form. Trust her, as she is a beautiful being."

After leaving the channeling state, I noticed a marked increase in my awareness of my spiritual friends. Their energy was noticeable to me at all times, and their voices guided me in the right direction. Sending a message of love and gratitude to my teacher, I felt a cool chill rush over my body, I knew he reciprocated.

PAST LIFE REGRESSION

In a hypnotic trance, I led my husband Andy through his memory of his days in the cavalry.

Walking into a fort that appeared unfinished, he felt excited and apprehensive at the same time. He noticed the men working to finish building the tall gates and some of the buildings that the cavalry officers and their families would live in.

Remembering our wedding day, he described me as wearing dark blue, rather than the traditional white. Feeling as if he didn't really know me very well, he was just happy to be marrying a woman that he felt was very pretty. A few years into the marriage, he felt that he was very happy. The two of us had gotten along very well, and it was working out. Pressing him forward, I asked him to recall the events that led to his learning of my affair.

Expressing physical discomfort, he saw himself sitting atop a horse on his way to battle. He felt angry, and said he no longer cared about his wife (me). On the battlefield, he described the carnage, the anguish clear in his voice. moments later, a total calm came over him and he said, "I don't feel a part of that scene anymore, I feel like I've turned upside down. I am watching from above, I feel like I might be dead."

Trying with no success to access the actual moment of finding out about Red Jacket, I slowly brought him out of his hypnotic trance. It was obviously too painful to deal with at that point.

HEAVENLY HAVENS

In the vibrational state, bordering on a very high dimension, I heard the voice of my teacher. The fear of seeing a ghost kept me from willing sight, and Emmanuel responded, "This is an important step, one that you must take. In order for you to grow in your abilities, you must rid yourself of the fear of ghosts.

Working up the courage, I willed sight. Dumbstruck by what I saw, Emmanuel responded, laughing, "See, it isn't so bad to see a ghost." Marveling at not only the beauty of the place I was in, but the feeling, I exclaimed, "*Oh, my God, this must be heaven, this really must be heaven!*" My beautiful teacher manifested himself in the same way he had to Theresia. Beautiful black hair of medium length, moustache and beard, a long white shimmering robe of light. What was most enthralling, however, were his beautiful, radiant eyes. His eyes held the deepest intensity I had ever seen, and all they could express was love.

Looking around at the dimension I inhabited for the moment, Emmanuel said, "This is where I often dwell, my dear." Bright colors, purples, pinks, and blues sashayed across the sky of lights. This dimension carried with it love, peace, and joy of indescribable proportions. Multi-colored sparklers filled the sky and the dimension shimmered with its beauty. Allowing myself to be swept up in the beauty and peace of the moment, I flew about like a bird with no need for wings!

Red Jacket appeared and told me that he needed to take me with him, holding out his hand I took it. Entering into a black tunnel with a bright light at the end, and exiting in the 19th century, Red Jacket dropped my spirit into the body of the woman I once was.

Immediately, I looked down. I was wearing a long dress with a petticoat and it felt heavy. Walking along the dirt roads, I was heading for a dingy bar, which was not more than an old barn with the front doors opened wide. Inside, my husband was arm wrestling with a group of men who were getting very rowdy. My husband was not a big man, he was a tad shorter than I, with straight sandy brown hair. The two men with him were quite large, and dirty. They both had wavy black hair, and a moustache. All the men seemed to be wearing clothes out of the television show "Gunsmoke." Dirty brown pants with suspenders and dingy shirts that used to be white. Some wore old hats, but most did not. My husband ordered me to leave as soon as he saw me, after all, this was no place for a woman and they were busy with menfolk talk. Angered by his reaction, I turned and left.

On my way back to our home, I passed by the prisoners' quarters, a building made of what appeared to be sandstone rock with one or two windows filled with black, metal bars.

Inside one of the windows, I saw the face of a young Indian boy and he motioned for me to come over. "We are very hungry, they do not feed us, can you help?" Compassion for this poor soul filled my being and I promised him that I would got food and return.

Upon return to the prison, I noticed the intoxicated condition of the two guards. One had fallen asleep and was laying in the dirt smelling strongly of whisky. The other stood tall against the prison wall in his blue cavalry uniform, holding his rifle upright, aiming for the sky. Bottle in hand, it wouldn't be long before he joined his friend on the ground. "Sir," I said with a curtsy, "I would just like to bring the prisoners some food for their bodies, and perhaps some food for their soul. I've prepared something for them to eat, and I know that they will be ready to hear about the Lord on a full stomach. I'd be mighty appreciative if you would let me help these poor souls enter into heaven." The guard flippantly moved away from the door and turned to unlock it. "Well, ma'am, that's mighty Christian of you, good luck to you, and God Bless!"

Walking into the door, and down a short flight of steps, I could not help but notice the disgustingly filthy conditions the Indians were being kept in. The prison was part underground and partly above, and the stone steps led into a small room (10' X 10') which housed about fifteen people. There were other cells, but I did not venture into them. Apparently, there were some prisoners who were kept in privately locked cells, and these were the most-wanted Indians.

The Indian boy, who could not be more than fifteen, was very appreciative that I had responded to his pleas. The others remained suspicious for a short time, until they could see that my intentions were good. While watching the Indian people eat their food, a decision was made within myself that this would not be the last time I fed them. I knew I had to return. As I began my ascent up the rock stairs, Red Jacket pulled me from the body, led me through the tunnel, and relinquished me into my present physical manifestation.

STEPS TO ENLIGHTENMENT

Emmanuel and my husband's guides were working with Andy to help him understand the importance of my journey.

One night, he had a dream that I wanted to buy myself a gift which consisted of a set of stairs and engraved porcelain fittings to piece onto each step. Each porcelain fitting was engraved with a spiritual concept I needed to embrace.

Andy did not want me to buy myself this gift, as he felt it was too expensive. The symbol here represented the amount of time I desired to spend on my journey.

His guides stepped in and told him that the steps represented my spiritual growth. Speaking in depth about the spiritual concepts I needed to learn, they made it clear to him that spiritual enlightenment was a most important gift to give myself, whatever the price.

Realizing its importance, Andy bought it for me as a birthday gift.

Upon returning from this dream, Andy's attitude changed immensely, as he had a better understanding of the real situation.

CHAPTER SIX
EMMANUEL

Emmanuel's first channeled sessions were a bit rough, and I took the liberty to edit them to avoid repetition and bad grammar. This is the first channeled session.

ONENESS

"Oneness is very important, as we are all a part of the whole. We very often do not recognize our existence as one.

When reflecting and thinking of other beings on the earth-plane, we often think in terms of "I" and "they." When we put other people down, we don't recognize that we are putting ourselves down. As a part of the whole, we are only as good as each of the parts. This is why those of us on the spiritual planes work so hard with those of you in the physical realms, to help raise the entire consciousness.

"For every consciousness that is raised, the whole, or the oneness, raises just a bit. If there was any way that one person could raise the whole consciousness of the earth just a tad, it would be by raising his own to a level beyond that what it is today. If it is higher tomorrow, the whole consciousness of the earth is raised just a bit.

"And, because we are all one, and we are all part of the network of the God-mind, the fact that this person had raised his consciousness would result in the continual growth of the God-consciousness. It would grow and grow daily, as that being was growing in his own oneness, consciousness, and spirituality.

The whole earth-plane would be raised because of the individual.

"This is why, when we are working with those who are raising their consciousness, and the oneness, we are able to work through them to help others raise their own consciousness. Even when you make the slightest move in that direction by helping one person remember one bit of truth that they had forgotten, just that tiny bit brings up the oneness of the earth-plane.

"Oneness is very important. Realize that everyone is one, and we are all an important part of the divine plan. Even the person perceived as the most loathsome entity on the earth-plane is just as important as you, me or any other entity. The highest evolutionary level entities are of no greater value than these on the lowest levels of the earth-plane.

"From the earth plane, there is great judgement. There is no need, as nothing is negative or positive, just growth-oriented, or non-growth oriented. And some actions that are growth-oriented for some, may not be for others. Some of these actions you may consider terrible, such as beings who experience the action of committing crimes, can be incredibly growth-oriented for an individual being.

"When we try to group people into bad and good, we overlook oneness, as we are all going to the same place, and that is home. Realizing this, we cannot judge anyone as bad, as that would be judging ourself. That person is going home, too.

There are times when your light can shine. This is not always the case as some choose a longer path. But there are times when your light can shine and turn another's direction. When your light shines changing that person's direction, as a part of the whole, it will change the entire consciousness of the earth plane."

NEW YORK, NEW YORK!

After leaving my body, I was whisked on a cloud to New York City. It was night, and the stars shone in the fairly clear night sky. The Empire State building loomed high above the skyline and I whizzed around the beautiful building. Flying high above the city, I enjoyed the beauty and soared peacefully.

After a short while, I went to New York University, though at the time, I did not know a college by that name existed. Cruising through the hallways, I watched students walking along on their way to classes, practice sessions, and home.

A performance was going on by the university band and choir, and I flew into the plant-filled auditorium where they played. Flying about, I spread my usual love vibrations to the packed room. Up in the bleachers, I sat down next to a family of four and let them wonder about my presence for a few minutes. After the performance was over, I cruised down the hallways feeling the grooves in the stone walls.

My first feeling about this, was that this trip to New York had something to do with my future. Later, I realized that I have a parallel lifetime going on in New York. Among other things, I would later visit the apartment and work place of this other self. A parallel lifetime is another lifetime that is going on in the same time-frame, but another reality. For example, if I chose to go to New York and find myself, I probably would not, as that "me" exists in another reality of this time period.

This sort of thing can be very confusing, but in the spiritual realm, time does not exist; therefore, you can exist at whatever time, place, or planet you choose. Even at the same "time," as time is an illusion, you can enter whatever reality you desire.

You may find that in the out-of-body state, I may describe experiences that seem to span a great deal more time than the "two hours" or so I may actually be gone from this plane of reality. Time only exists in dimensions where it is created as a structure to enable the function of society.

When you leave your body, you also leave behind that structure of time.

Time is like a kaleidoscope when seen from the eternal. It stands before you as a menu of what options you may choose from, which realities will serve you, and bring you to greater light. You may leave this time-frame, and return in any time-frame that serves a purpose to your growth.

Whether it be time-travel to peer at other lifetimes which hold secrets to your present, or, having the capability to return to your body after lengthy excursions into light, at a time compatible with the point of reference you left that form. . .your present physical lifestyle will always remain intact and working smoothly. For most of us, our guides will lead us to return within a few hours of our departure. Otherwise, our bodies could appear to be comatose for two weeks or more, earth time. . .which is not usually for our highest good in this realm (though sometimes it may be, as in Jack London's *The Star Rover*, where remaining comatose for long periods actually kept a tortured prisoner alive).

Time and timelessness: it's all relative, and this is why we can do it.

BEAMING DOWN FROM VENUS

Theresia told my friend Marilyn that she felt I was beaming down from Venus, which seemed intriguing.

Then, Emmanuel was pushing me to find out more about a pendant he wore. Theresia, in her drawing, depicted Emmanuel as wearing the astrological sign of Taurus the Bull around his neck. Since I had no idea what any of this meant, I asked Theresia.

When I first asked her, she did not understand the connection, but a day or so later, she called to tell me that she had remembered that these two signs were connected with the second coming of the Christ Consciousness. Channeling Emmanuel for more understanding, he spoke about this, as well as my husband's problem with insomnia.

THE CHRIST CONSCIOUSNESS

"Hello. This is Emmanuel. Marilynn, you are beaming down from Venus. And this means that you have had much time to evolve.

"At this time you have chosen to come back to help in the second coming of the Christ Consciousness. We term it "beaming down from Venus," because these spirits on Venus will be inhabiting that reality in another way in the future in greater quantities, and are all spirits who have evolved greatly. Many of whom, have returned in physical form to be "discipled" in the second coming of the Christ Consciousness.

"This will be done in many ways. There are healers, teachers, those working in smaller ways with friends and family, and those who have chosen to be a larger voice. As a larger voice, you will learn to channel, our energies will become intertwined and much stronger together, and you will bear some of the messages of the Christ consciousness. And you will do this for people that I choose to bring to you.

"You need patience, as you are but an infant in your opening. You need to develop and open more, and we need to synchronize our energies. Over a short period of time, you will develop channeling, hearing, seeing, and we will be able to communicate one-on-one with you. This is what we agreed to prior to your existence here on the earth-plane.

"The second coming will be a consciousness-raising. Many beings will reach higher levels of consciousness, others will stay behind. As the ones who stay behind will not be compatible with these who go forward, some will choose to join the spiritual society on Venus. Nothing drastic will happen, just that those who choose to grow will reach the inevitable end of their lifetime here and choose not to return. And as a result of the rising consciousness of the earth, this planet will be more conducive to growth as well.

"You must be patient, as you will not be able to complete your goals, unless you allow us on the spiritual plane, to continue our work with you.

"With Andy's question about his inability to sleep, I am being told by his guides that they need him to ask. They want him to ask with meaning, and to believe in their existence and their presence, so they may help him.

"There is past-life significance which he must delve into with his guides, a lifetime he may not be aware of at this point. He must desire to sleep better and to communicate with his guides. They have a desire to communicate with him. He still has trouble, though he is doing quite admirably in challenging old beliefs, in feeling these new experiences as more than a concept, and as a reality.

"His guides speak to him, but they go unheard. He has a hard time accepting his intuition and instincts, which are really the voices of his own guides. He must take a step in that direction.

"Andy needs to take more time with his growth than you, Marilynn. He values caution, you value speed. He feels that he must see or hear something earth-shattering to believe it is the word of his guides. If he hears a voice, he will automatically claim it as his own, then feeling it not important because it is his own thought. He sees this as a concept, rather than reality.

"He will reach that point, and soon. When he feels he can take that dramatic step forward, he will begin to unravel the mystery of this lifetime. The important thing for him to do now, is to ask, ask, and ask, again. If he hears, but he doesn't understand, he needs to ask for greater understanding. His guides are ready, willing, and able to help him, and they love him very much. They love him very, very, much! They want contact, and they will have it because he wants it, too.

"He needs to break through that belief center that says it is just not possible, and once that belief is disbanded, he will open to the universe, and he will grow. This is because he will then *see* the reality, and it will no longer be a concept."

THE SPECTATOR

While leaving my body, I noticed something odd. Looking down at my bed from another dimension, I noticed that there were two "Andy's."

Andy was out of his body, also, and undergoing a vibration raising. His physical body lay on the bed, and his etheric body was raised just above it, vibrating rapidly. A spiritual guide at his side, like an electrical technician, was overseeing the raising. Watching the affair, Emmanuel spoke to me, telling me to inform Andy of this incident, as he would not remember it. They wanted him to know that they were working with him. Agreeing to tell him, I whizzed off to my next destination.
. .

RED JACKET REUNION

After undergoing a vibrational raising of my own, I went to a coliseum-like place crowded with entities waiting to hear a speaker. The coliseum was round, with basketball-like bleachers all around, and a huge podium was in the middle. Realizing that this was not the astral plane, I assumed it to be another dimension I had not yet traversed.

Sitting down, I felt intense love directed at me coming from behind, and it felt very nice. Turning to see who the source of this love was, I saw a man who was large, Roman-looking, with sandy-blonde hair looking at me with incredible recognition. Feelings were there, but I could not place them, I did not recognize this entity. I turned back to listen to the speaker who was just about to begin.

Thousands of entities were in attendance, and the feminine entity speaking began to talk of spiritual teachers, and what their role was. The intensity of the love feelings from behind me was growing, and the speaker seemed to notice it, too. Immediately beaming over to where I was sitting, all eyes were suddenly on me. With a smile, she asked me to turn around.

The same man was sitting there, but slowly his image began to change. Long black hair, olive skin, a headband around his forehead, it was Red Jacket! Overcome with emotion, I began to cry tears of joy. He came over to embrace me, his joy obvious, and the crowd went wild at our reunion of love. Reaching out my hand to Red Jacket, in a flash of light, we left the coliseum.

Moments later, we were in a beautiful forest. The trees were all green with their summer leaves, and we sat down in the brush and embraced. Reveling in each other's presence, we didn't speak. Amazed at the powerful love this Indian had for me, I was overcome with emotion and the illusion I had created in our lifetime together was totally shattered. No doubt existed as to the reality of our love. At that moment, it was all that was.

A few months later, I would learn that the original manifestation of Red Jacket in the coliseum was that of another life that we spent together. Via the time tunnel, I would relive that life.

WHAT'S A WALL, ANYWAY?

Journeying inward to another plane of existence, I met Emmanuel in an unoccupied home in a suburban area.

Stating that I had blocks that I needed to work through regarding the permeation of physical objects, he presented me with the "Emmanuel physical illusion workout." This consisted of flying through the ceiling over and over again, until I got through it.

The first few tries, I could not get through the ceiling. Emmanuel, in his ultimate patience, just sat there and told me to do it over, until I could permeate it. After succeeding in flying through the ceiling, he asked me to do it several times more, until I felt certain I had overcome this block. Upon succeeding with that, he took me back to my home.

Outside, he showed me a thought-form. My neighbor was mowing his lawn with a four or five-year-old boy. Their son was presently a young baby. Emmanuel said that this was the space of time when some of my goals would be met. I returned to my body.

Another night, Emmanuel channeled through to help my husband while I was astral. Andy was trying his new relaxation exercises and feeling warm waves of energy coming through him. After a short time, he felt he had lost the connection completely. Emmanuel said, "Hey!" and with that word, his body was completely energized! Meanwhile, I was spying on some friends in North Carolina!

TEACH ME ABOUT TEACHERS

Emmanuel led me to a meeting at a local metaphysical book store. Hoping to meet some nice people and tell them about my great friend, Emmanuel, I went with high expectations.

An older black woman was there "teaching" the class, and from the moment I walked in the door, she didn't like my presence.

She said a lot of things that I felt were false, and I stated my feelings. While she told those in the group that their own impressions of their experiences were false, I interrupted and stated that only the one who has the experience or dream can truly know its meaning.

Her anger intensified and she was throwing insults my way. Sarcastically, she called me "prophet," and told me I could not handle being around her "high vibration." Ego structure was the highest thing in the room.

This was a lesson to me that you should never give your power away to a teacher, as the only master of you, is you. Realizing, also, that becoming a teacher was not my purpose, as Emmanuel had other plans for me. The sad part of this story is that the woman probably began teaching with all good intentions, but allowed her ego to grow, rather than herself, thus stifling her own spiritual growth to maintain her "teacher" status. Our journey is always inward, not outward.

LITTLE CHINAMAN

Andy had a dream about a little Chinaman. He saw himself in a room that contained an imaginary line, bordering on another dimension.

Suddenly, a small man with short, black hair came through that imaginary line, and Andy immediately recognized him.

"Little Chinaman, you're here!" he said, as the little being quietly giggled and jumped back over the line.

Andy was frightened by the appearance of the harmless little being, and the being sensed this. Hopping out of sight, Little Chinaman did not want to scare him.

In Virginia Beach on vacation at the time of this incident, Andy had been talking in his sleep about oneness. On that vacation, we were also surprised to find "Emmanuel's Book" by Pat Rodegast. We wondered if our Emmanuel was the same entity.

ENERGY ALIGNMENT

Having over-exerted myself during our vacation, my asthma condition had worsened.

Entering into the vibratory state, I left my body. Suddenly seeing from another vantage point, my etheric body was displayed before my eyes. An obvious energy disturbance could be seen in my chest area, a discoloration. Resembling thermal photography, my consciousness was displayed as a white light with a red color emanating from the area of disease.

Realizing the need to deal with my lung condition more thoroughly, I worked on refining the energy. As I brought my energy pattern back to balance, I knew I would need to work on understanding my disease, and the creation of it.

UTE

Cruising in the out-of-body state, I materialized in a veterans' hospital for a handicapped man.

The man was very young, attractive, handicapped, and depressed. He had a bandage around his forehead with only a small amount of his medium, brown hair showing.

Apparently, he felt unloved and had few visitors, until now! We talked for quite a while, small talk mostly, but he felt the love that I had to offer. Suddenly, he looked at me with confusion and said, "You aren't from here, are you, Ute? Like, I mean, your a spirit, aren't you?" I didn't know how to respond, and I didn't have to, as Red Jacket pulled me immediately out of the scene. To the soldier, I just disappeared.

"Ute?" I asked Red Jacket ponderously. "Why did he call

me Ute?" Red Jacket laughed and said, "Because that is who you are!"

I returned to my body and wrote down the name. Looking in the dictionary, I was surprised to find that the definition of Ute is an important tribe of the Shoshonean stock of North American Indians now on reservations in Utah and Colorado.

Red Jacket had been an Ute Indian in our lifetime together, and I also found that I had been an Ute Indian in the past. My history was unfolding!

When pursuing your spiritual path, the most important aspect is a true and strong desire. In the creation of reality, it is the strength and intensity of the emotion behind the thought-forms you create, which are the driving force of manifestation. And as you enter into the realms of contact, the next important step is to open your eyes. In order to enter into total understanding and love, one must strive to dissolve the ego, which is the greatest block to seeing truth.

To learn to truly, not conceptually, love unconditionally is the goal of all spiritual concepts. Unconditional love is a feeling, an emotion. It is also the ability to put the world in the hands of the divine plan, and know that everything will be alright.

CHAPTER SEVEN

LESSONS IN LOVE

ACCEPTANCE

Emmanuel on love:
"Love is the greatest emotion of all, as it expresses all that is. Love in its purest form is the greatest healer, the greatest power and the only energy force in the universe.

The state of love is the highest vibratory state one can be in. In that state, you are expressing the knowing of all things.

"Those who learn to truly love, see the value of all things, all people, all souls. From the spectacle of love, they see that all paths are equal, no act is good or bad, it merely is. Seeing things from the perspective of love is acceptance.

"Acceptance is an important part of growth. Accepting everyone's reality as their own, that all realities are equal to yours, that their path is necessary for them, and that all must find truth in their own time.

"Love is unconditional acceptance, truly valuing what someone is and what someone is not. If you truly value these qualities that you perceive as good, and these qualities that you perceive as bad, thus accepting the whole, then you are truly loving. That is good.

"In order to love yourself, you must enter acceptance. Most judge their own behavior such as irrationality, ego, and anger, and they don't feel good about themselves. The reality is, self-love means accepting these moments of irrationality, lack-of-judgment, or hurting another's feelings as part of you. For until you accept them as part of you, they will never change. All love begins with acceptance, and with acceptance, there can be growth!"

INSTANCE OF ACCEPTANCE

In another dimension, I met an old friend from years back.

About ten years prior, we had gone to school together, been cruel to each other as many children are, and were returning to work things out.

Talking about our feelings, he apologized for the cruelty and told me that he loved me very much. When he was through, we embraced, and it was over. All that remained was unconditional love. Enjoying the space we occupied for a short time, we lovingly said goodbye, and went our separate ways.

Upon return to the physical, I felt strong love for this person who I literally had not thought of for ten years. That tiny piece of karma was worked out, and we had reached the light of unconditional love.

At the time, I did not understand what that experience meant, but in a short while, it became a common occurrence with clear intent.

I came to call these reunions of love-stockpile experiences, as I had developed a huge pile of rejections and hurts throughout this lifetime. Most appeared small and unimportant at the time, but apparently, each hurt stayed with me subconsciously. Dealing with it required understanding, forgiveness, and the realization that the hurt did not denote a lack of love. It is the physical illusion, the limited nature, and the ego, that drives someone to hurt another. Our own lack of self-love allows us to strike out at others, and this is misunderstood as rejection. At the core of every being, lies the light of unconditional love. Anyone who displays hate is displaying their illusion, because in our unlimited form love is all there is. The goal of these experiences, then, was to remove each individual from my rejection stockpile, thus opening me to more love and more dimensions of reality. Over a period of several months, I would meet with many people from my past, and eventually, from past lives, bringing back the only important aspect of our relationships, love. Meeting with several beings every night, I included only a few of the hundreds of stockpile meetings.

A PRAIRIE RENDEZVOUS

Meeting with Red Jacket, he smiled and took me to another reality. A beautiful prairie, tumbleweeds blowing by, and a majestic mountain ahead, we climbed onto two horses. Riding into the sunset, we enjoyed the peaceful spectacle of the west.

To the side of us, a third horse appeared with a young Indian boy riding, our beautiful son. Smiling at us, the young boy waved good-bye and disappeared as quickly as he came.

Feeling so utterly joyful, I drew my horse closer to Red Jacket and hopped on the back of his horse, setting mine free. Red Jacket raised his right arm, and we were no longer in that space.

Around a campfire, I sat in a state of being as Red Jacket looked at me from above. The campfire gleamed light onto my surroundings, as I noticed I was a female Indian. Two tepees could be seen clearly in the firelight, off-white with a reddish jagged line painted around the bottom, and I could see that there were many more shadowed by the night. Directly behind me, a beautiful forest serenaded me with the sounds of the wind blowing through the branches and the night animals calling. Red Jacket smiled as I realized that this was somewhere I had once lived. Lovingly, he took my hand and brought me back to my present reality.

Red Jacket and I had worked through our hurts and reached unconditional love. By discarding the separate horses, and joining together on the same path, we set our past free, and began our ascent to the future.

EMMANUEL ON SELF-LOVE

EMMANUEL: (Laughing)

ANDY: Why are you laughing?

EMMANUEL: It's fun to be here, again. (Laughing)

ANDY: It's nice to have you here. How can I get in better touch with my guides?

EMMANUEL: You already are in good touch with your guides, you simply do not realize it. Little Chinaman is trying to make better contact.

ANDY: Can you tell me more about Little Chinaman?

EMMANUEL: He is your teacher, and he's been working with you on many issues, which is difficult because of your own lack of belief in yourself.

ANDY: How can I learn to believe in myself better?

EMMANUEL: First, you must know that you are a part of God, and truly believe it. It is difficult to realize one's own value, when comparing yourself to others in the earth-plane. These beings, more often than not, are much less evolved than yourself. You are no less evolved than your wife, but you do not see that, as she is more aware at this moment in time. Having traveled many roads together, you are not inferior simply because she has accessed more of her inner abilities. You have not realized your own power, and you need to realize that what you are is good. When you doubt yourself, you do not move forward. When you compare yourself with others, you drag yourself deeper into the physical illusion.

When you choose to believe in yourself, know that you are a part of God, and that your guides are there, you can move forward in your own awareness. Your guides are very excited about your impending awareness of their existence.

ANDY: I don't quite understand how I can become more aware. EMMANUEL: You must want it. If you don't truly want it, that is okay. In order to grow you must truly have the desire. Let Little Chinaman feel your desire, and he will help you move forward. If you have questions, ask them. Really listen to your own inner guidance, as it comes from your higher self and your guides. Trust your instincts.

ANDY: I would like to know more about Little Chinaman.

EMMANUEL: Little Chinaman and you shared past lives. You remember him as Little Chinaman, because you were little Chinamen together (laughing). Subconsciously you remember him well. As great friends, he reached mastery and you moved onto other lifetimes. He has been with you ever since.

ANDY: What can we do to help our daughter be more spiritual? (pause) Or should we do anything at all?

EMMANUEL: Good distinction! With Melissa at her present age (14 months) the best thing you can do for her, is to let her have fun and enjoy the spirituality of being a child. As she grows, encourage inward growth. All children are born with innate truth, but are told to forget it. She will be more aware simply because she is never forced to forget. Allow her to be who she is, even if it disagrees with your own truth.

ANDY: Why was I so afraid when I saw Little Chinaman?

EMMANUEL: Part of the fear would be the inevitable fear of reaching into the spiritual realm, with the programming that it is a scary and dangerous place to be. There are other blocks, too, that must be dealt with individually with Little Chinaman.

ANDY: I appreciate you talking to me about these things. Thank you.

EMMANUEL: I am happy to do it. Those of us in the spiritual realm, work with those where you exist because it is fun, which is the best reason to do anything. We gain just as much by helping you, as you gain by receiving it.

ANDY: This may not be a good question, but. . .

EMMANUEL: All questions are good.

ANDY: I'd like to know where my Grandpa is? (He had died a few years earlier.)

EMMANUEL: My images are not yet clear. I feel he is still in the learning phase. He is very close to the physical realm, as he spends much time with your grandmother. Much of his time is spent learning things he neglected to learn while on earth. What I am feeling is that he is in the spiritual plane, but has not yet moved onto a new program. While learning about the universe, he is waiting for your grandmother to join him. After people die, many choose to hang around the edge of the two worlds to observe their loved ones. They may not move on until certain loved ones finish their life and join them.

ANDY; Thank you.

EMMANUEL: You're welcome.

ANDY: I still have problems with insomnia. I have used the ideas you gave me and they have helped considerably. Are there any more to add?

EMMANUEL: The key for you is to totally let go of all your worries, as there are many varied things that plague your mind. Let go of the physical illusion, and allow yourself to be drawn into the spiritual realm. Allow your mind to be clear, so that we may enter. Ask Little Chinaman, and listen when he answers.

It is difficult in a physical body to know when you are being spoken to, as it may be just a little voice in your head, or a sudden answer to a problem that you have wondered about. Usually, you wonder why you didn't think of it sooner, as it was so simple, but the reality is that truth *is* simple. Allow yourself to pay more attention, and accept your guide's presence. Know that there is more in the universe than you are presently aware of, and desire to learn of it. Ask, and feel it.

Once you understand things from a truer perspective, looking down at the earth from a high vantage point, rather than
from the ground up, the triviality of your illusion will become
clear. The earth is a school and a passing place, understand
that. Seeing your illusion from that perspective will allay the
worries that keep you from sleeping, as they will no longer
seem important.

ANDY: Thank you for talking with me, I look forward to
speaking with you again.

EMMANUEL: As I with you. . .

BLOCKS TO INNER TRUTH

Undergoing a very intense vibrational raising, Emmanuel
reminded me that my journey was to be inward. Trying to lift
out, I was prevented from doing so.

As I continued to transmute the energies into my being, I
focused intently on traveling inward to another dimension.

Realizing that I was not allowing myself to see, my fear was
preventing any journey.

The rejection stockpile was too large! In order for me to
experience those other exciting and extremely loving dimensions, I had to work through the subconscious hurts that told
me I was not worthy, that I was not loved. Once I could
eliminate that pile, I would be free!

Recently, I had reached the point of remembering my entire
sleep-life consciously, a goal I had desired. Meeting many of
my stockpile friends, I was learning just how important even
the smallest hurts can be, and each reunion released just a little
more light into my being. With each hurt, I had blocked out
just a tiny bit of light, or love from God, and now I was
restoring my being to its original state. These seemingly small
hurts are your subconscious blocks that are preventing your
growth.

If you would like to address your own stockpile, you can,
as you can communicate telepathically in your physical form
to the entities in your own pile. Being totally honest about
your feelings is essential, and even if the other being does not
respond consciously, they will subconsciously. This may help
to spur more conscious awareness at night, as you are consciously dealing with your blocks to light. The goal in your
communication will be to remove the hate, hurt, confusion,

and anger, and leave nothing but love. It is this love that brought you together in the first place. All negative behavior is brought on by the illusion as reality is love. The pain you feel is real, but the conclusion is a falsehood. As love is all there is, it is incorrect to conclude that you are not loved.

LAKE CROSSINGS

In a thought-form reality, a dream-like astral experience that we create to teach ourselves, I entered a small town on the edge of a lake. Feeling drawn to the lake, I created a thought-form bus to take me to it. The bus was crowded, so I stood throughout the long ride, and each moment, the longing to reach the lake increased.

When I got off the bus and looked at the lake, I felt an incredible familiarity, and I knew that I had been there before.

The lake front was very built up with one- and two-story brick buildings surrounding the tiny beach. Sitting down to look at the beautiful lake, a man tapped my shoulder, and I turned.

Immediately recognizing the being, I realized this was a stockpile visit. He was the very best friend in the world to me at one time. My feelings were more intense, however, and believing it to be mutual, was quite shocked when I found that he had another girlfriend who was pregnant.

Lovingly, my friend explained something to me that would become a recurring theme in many of my stockpile experiences: misunderstanding. Our relationship was not official, we had no commitment, and I gave him mixed signals. Due to my upbringing, I was afraid to be vulnerable to anyone, because they could reject me, thus, reinforcing my feeling of being unlovable. My actions, however, made others feel rejected and they would not approach me. Therefore, my fear was realized anyway, as my "safety valve" created the reality I desired to avoid.

Reassuring me that he did love me very much, just as he loved the other woman, I asked him to clarify the difference. "Love is love," he said, "it cannot be classified." That made sense to me, and I pondered this truth as we sat together. "I think I understand," I said, "as love exists as a feeling and emotion, you cannot limit its intensity by labeling it. In a state of oneness, the same intensity can be felt for all life. He embraced me and turned to leave. I jumped back onto my thought-form bus, which took me to a house right outside of town. It was a two-story, red-brick house built on a hill and surrounded by acres of grassy earth.

Remembering this home, I walked into the thought-form building and looked around. A man wearing all black clothing was working on carpentry, and a woman was doing needlepoint in another room. This woman was myself in a past life. I knew her to be a servant, and she hated the man in the other room. Not knowing why, I left this thought-form reality, and returned to my body.

In our illusion, we box our love into categories and limited definitions. In reality, love is too vast to be contained. Feeling love for other beings does not diminish love for the one, it expands it. If you remove someone's freedom to love others, you remove their freedom to love you, too.

A HELPING HAND

In a conscious sleep-state, I felt three fingers touch my forehead by my sixth chakra, filling me with energy. Emmanuel was charging my batteries and it lasted about ten minutes. As the experience was very soothing, I reveled in it as long as I could absorbing this energy wand.

INDIAN WAYS

In a dream, Red Jacket showed me a book that he wanted me to read about the Ute Indians. Finding it a week or two later, the book was entitled *War Cry on a Prayer Feather*, by Nancy Wood, and it contained poems and writings of Ute Indians. Remembrance came over my being as I read the book, feeling the oneness of the Indian society. What a shame that the white man was so arrogant to believe that they could tame the Indians, when it was they who were the savages.

In the meantime, my stockpile had lowered considerably, as I met with old friends, boyfriends, and other seemingly insignificant acquaintances. Returning from these experiences, I felt only love for those I met. Despite my former feelings of anger, resentment or hurt, upon return, all illusions were resolved, forever! Part of the excitement is knowing that they were really there, too, regardless of whether they remember it consciously.

ENTITY, ENTITY, GO AWAY

In a sleep-state a lost soul's death scene began to play over and over. Horrifying as it seemed, I was determined to keep it in perspective and not allow fear to enter my reality.

The woman was working in a nuclear power plant standing outside by one of the large, looming towers. Suddenly, an explosion was heard, a fire ensued, and people were running towards her. Another explosion went off, and before she had a chance to run, a third, which took her life. Having been completely blown up, she was extremely traumatized.

The death was gruesome, and I fought the fear that came with it by determining that I would see this from the spiritual reality, rather than the physical illusion. Beginning telepathic communication, I realized part of her shock was due to her own involvement in the explosion, as she felt she was the cause. Sharing my love with her, I told her that everything was going to be alright, despite the horrible suffering she had endured.

Explaining the reality beyond the physical and about the light, and her guides, she calmed down immensely, with an understanding of this exciting, loving universe. "You mean I won't be judged for what I did, even though it took all these lives?" she said. "God loves you, honey, and there isn't anything you could do to turn him away. His love is complete, it is unconditional." I told her to stick around me as long as necessary, but that when she was ready, her guides would be there to take her to the light. Half an hour later she turned to meet her loving friends.

As death is just another physical illusion, it is necessary to remove yourself from the physical interpretation of havoc and horror. The lost soul is not a symbol of that horror, as he/she no longer inhabits his/her limited form. In the unlimited form, he/she represents the love of God, and it is essential that one is reunited with that love.

EMMANUEL ON TEACHING

Having asked Emmanuel whether I should teach others at

this time, he responded with something I think we can all benefit from hearing:

"In order to grow, one must learn to bask in solitude. To you, the knowledge you have gained seems commonplace. To others it is crazy. Having been shown many wonders of reality, you feel a need to share that with others. However, if everyone understood all that is, then the illusion would be unnecessary. Many beings have chosen to block out all reality in their illusion, completely. For you to awaken them would not be beneficial, and, frankly, it will not happen. Some beings are in a state where they need that totality of illusion. They will do as their paths enable them to do, and you will reach only those who are ready to hear.

"Many teachers, in their excitement at their first glance at spirituality, run to tell the world, thus, they cease to continue their own growth, as it is the ego that desires to teach others of its incredible knowledge. In your new place, you feel rejection by churches and other less-aware beings, and your ego says, Let me demonstrate to you how much I know so that I may gain your acceptance and respect.' Some will see your truth, but some will see you as evil, due to their own fears.

"It is precisely this action that forces you to choose your spiritual growth or your ego, as you cannot truly have both. Your ego desires to be recognized, but your spirituality will not always be recognized by others, as they cannot see your bright light.

"Know that in your ultimate state of unconditional love, your light can be spread, not by words, but by example. It is a perfect plan."

That evening, while lying awake in bed, Emmanuel appeared as purple and green lights dancing across my ceiling. Calming and beautiful, it was his first appearance to me in the physical realm.

CHAPTER EIGHT

HEART OF THE HORSE

A CHAT WITH EMMANUEL

Projecting into another dimension with my subconscious astral husband, we prepared to speak with Emmanuel. The dimension we occupied was somewhat foggy, as a cloudy haze surrounded everything, but the light was immense. Sitting down in anticipation of meeting this great being, we spoke of how honored we felt to have such a superior entity as our friend.

When Emmanuel arrived, however, he appeared to us in a very ordinary way. Rather than the robe of light I had previously seen, he manifested himself in street clothes. Laughing a bit, he said, "Do not make me more than I am. As I am divine energy, so are you. Do not glorify me." Knowing that it was time for us to go, we thanked him for the message. "We will meet many more times, my friends," he said, as we went our separate ways. Leaving Andy back in his body, I projected into another lifetime.

Dropped into the body of a male Indian, I was living on a volcanic mountain with my small child. The child's mother was dead.

It was a peaceful and sunny day that ended in disaster, as the volcanic mountain that our tribe lived on began erupting with a fury. Smoke and lava began to spew effortlessly down the mountain, killing many in its wake. Located two miles from the crater, I knew the only hope was to climb on top of a large boulder to avoid the lava streams. With every moment, the sky became darker with ash and smoke.

After the eruption was over, we spent several weeks surviving any way we could as we ventured down the stricken volcano. Few from our tribe survived the eruption, and we had to accept that our tribal society was finished. As the mountain vegetation was burned, our best option was to live among the white people in a small town not too far away.

Feeling misplaced, we adjusted to their ways of life as well as we could. When asked, I would explain our ways, but they had trouble understanding the simplicity. We lived in small spaces and we were one, but most of all, we were very happy. Returning to my body, I longed for that mountain.

STOCKPILE STUPOR

In a stockpile reunion, I ran into a new problem. Meeting in a bare dimension, which could only be described as empty space, a former friend of mine appeared.

Ready to confront all the hurt feelings, I told her how, despite it all, I loved her. She responded in vicious anger, "You're just a drag, and I can't stand you!"

Our friendship had broken up when I met my husband, as she felt that I no longer spent enough time with her. After a long fun-filled friendship, she no longer spoke to me because I had chosen to get married.

"You are not ready to let this go and that's okay. I, however, am ready. I love you very much and the illusion is not reality to me." Leaving the scene, I knew that someday we would meet again when she was ready to reduce her own stockpile.

The important thing was for me to work through my own stockpile, regardless of whether she could. When she was ready to let go, we would meet again.

MY INDIAN NAME

Traveling astrally towards a beautiful mountain range in the distance, Red Jacket spoke behind me. We followed a two-lane road which was sparsely traveled by cars. Three mountains were in clear sight, two small ones surrounding a huge, snow-capped beauty in the middle. "There is a being," he said, "who is at one with these mountains. The animals and the trees are her friends, and she speaks with all life. In her heart, she has lived here for centuries."

Reaching the bottom edge of the huge mountain, Red Jacket directed me to fly up the slopes. Halfway up the mountain, a beautiful horse was carved in the bluish rock, which appeared to be in motion.

Immediately I soared to the midsection of the horse and listened to its heartbeat. "And you, my friend, are Heart of the Horse! It is your name, it is your legacy." The being that Red Jacket spoke about was me. Feeling joyful, I returned to my body.

Later, while reading a book on the Indian ways, I found that the horse represents the new way, thus, my name meant "heart of the new way."

GLOBE OF LIGHT

Meeting an old friend from my high school marching band in the empty space, we found that we shared the same teacher, Emmanuel. We had been casual friends, as he dated a friend of mine.

No stockpile existed, and we just discussed reality and metaphysics. Great love was felt between us, and we enjoyed just being together.

Emmanuel came in, and I waved good-bye, following my teacher to our next destination, which was a spot in the empty space reality.

Having my vibrations raised, I transmuted the energy into my being, taking occasional breaks to go home and peek at my husband and daughter playing together in the afternoon.

In a short while, however, the intensity of the experience exploded, as I began to see a globe of purple and white light rotating expressively through my consciousness.

Realizing this as the center of my being, the globe rotated and flew about my mind as it absorbed the intense light. For a moment, I wondered if I had passed on, as I could not break the energy current and return to my body. Several minutes later, I returned feeling energized and peaceful, a calm hum felt throughout my being. *Talk about vibes!*

My stockpile continued to dwindle, as I met many different beings. An interesting twist occurred when I met someone I had loved very much, who didn't reciprocate. Despite this, he was hurt that I had moved on. He had assumed I would always be there. We were able to relinquish our illusion to the underlying love. Another case involved a former neighbor, who was tense whenever we were together. This had made me feel disliked, and we worked through some of the hard feelings, but not completely.

Every stockpile problem has different facets and hurts to work through. Allow yourself time to deal with each one, and enjoy these beautiful reunions of love. Every incident in your life will be addressed. If someone walked across the street and called you a name, you will meet them. Having met about a hundred of my own stockpile friends, you can be sure that you will have many, too.

SPIRIT GAMES

After listening to knocking sounds on the bathroom window, scraping sounds outside, and our stereo blaring when I returned from the store only to shut off as I opened the door, I knew it could only be Emmanuel or Red Jacket. Perhaps I had not been paying enough attention to them lately? Hearing a noise behind me, I saw a wispy figure of Red Jacket speed by. It was time to channel.

EMMANUEL ON MEDITATION

EMMANUEL: Hello, am I disturbing you?

ANDY: No. You are not. I haven't talked to you in a while because I felt there was a lot for me to do with what we talked about in our last conversation.

EMMANUEL: Any progress?

ANDY: In terms of convictions, yes, but otherwise, I don't think so. I'm trying to be patient.

EMMANUEL: Persistence.

ANDY: I haven't seen Chinaman since our last visit, and I am wondering what I can do to strengthen our connection.

EMMANUEL: Desire it.

ANDY: I guess it is true that I have not desired it a lot, lately, I am not sure what to ask him.

EMMANUEL: Perhaps it's not what you ask, but that you ask. Ask him to show you what is real. There is much for you to learn about what things really are, as opposed to, what they appear to be. Make a conscious effort to see the reality in all things, rather than the physical interpretation, as that will open doors.

There is still much fear for you in opening those doors. In your lifetime in the cavalry, you suffered much pain. Consciously re-feeling that pain is frightening to you, but you must understand it, so that you may bring it to the light of love.

ANDY: Can you tell me what these hurts and pains were?

EMMANUEL: Not at this time. Take your steps one at a time, and ask Little Chinaman to help you.

ANDY: How will Little Chinaman manifest himself to me. Will I see lights?

EMMANUEL: I don't believe he plans to manifest that way. I manifest through color, but every spirit chooses different means. This is a good time to begin meditation on a regular basis, as this will unlock doors into the spiritual realm.

You have a great need to understand the truth, and until this occurs, it will be difficult for you to work through your past. Viewing your lives from the light of unconditional love requires an ability to see from the spiritual realm.

ANDY: Thank you for giving me these answers.

EMMANUEL: You are very welcome.

ANDY: How will I know when I make contact with my guide?

EMMANUEL: When it happens, you will know. Trust your instincts, as until you listen to the messages that come through you without doubts, contact will not be made. We are in contact with everyone in the physical realm, but most have no idea, as they explain everything away. Perhaps a rapping on a window (laughing) is just our way of getting your attention. When you hear a message, don't doubt it. Allow it into your life.

Meditation will help you to increase your conscious aware-ness of Little Chinaman. Meditation is initial contact. Talk to him like a friend, even if you feel silly. Know that they hear you, and that you are opening doors.

We want to contact you just as much as you want to contact us, as I am sure you can see by some of our drastic means (laughing).

ANDY: I'm happy that you want to contact me.

EMMANUEL: We are happy that you want to contact us! Make a conscious effort to remove your subconscious fears, so that we may contact you personally. Remember that there is nothing to fear and no harm will come to you. You have been taught to fear the spiritual realm, and there is no neces-sity for fear.

ANDY: What should I do when I meditate?

EMMANUEL: Relax your body and focus your mind on one concept. Focus on something so simple and yet so vast, as love. Concentrate on that as you go deeper into the meditative state, and understanding will come to you.

ANDY: Should I think of relationships or experiences I have had with love?

EMMANUEL: Just think love. Love is much more vast than you are presently aware, as it is all things. It may seem vague to you, but in the meditative state, your guides will help you access your higher understanding.

Trust the messages that come to you during meditation, and as the concepts and ideas flow through, take new avenues and expand on another aspect of the concept (laughing)! Do you understand?

ANDY: Should I meditate before I go to bed, or should I set aside a time every day to meditate?

EMMANUEL: You can do both, or either. Find time to meditate in your slow moments at the office. Quiet your mind, go into the inner recesses of your soul, and energize your being! If you recall, your wife started with meditation and self-hypnosis. You must take the beginning steps when tapping the energy of the universe.

Do it when you feel like it, do not box yourself in. It is important to have fun.

My connection is weakening, and I must go. Thank you very much for speaking with me, and we all love you very much.

ANDY: I love you, too.

EMMANUEL: Thanks for having us. Little Chinaman says hi! ANDY: I FEEL HIM!

LITTLE CHINAMAN

Swept through the dark tunnel of time, I was dropped into the lifetime that Andy spent with Little Chinaman.

Little Chinaman was an aging master, almost bald, very thin and somber. Andy was a young Chinese, with jet black hair that would shine in the light, a beautiful smile, and very tall and muscular. They lived together in Little Chinaman's small, two-bedroom home, where he taught others mastery. Paying the master back by taking care of the home, Andy was Little Chinaman's prize student and friend.

In the front room of the home, I and two other students sat discussing our lessons. Feeling a strong attraction to Andy, as I was a Chinese woman, I got up from the table and went to speak with him. Upon my approach, his aura became bright red and yellow, the anger obvious. My presence made him very angry, as the subconscious memory of our previous life with Red Jacket plagued him.

Having been left in charge of our lessons by Little Chinaman, Andy immediately responded to my presence by ordering me to do physical labor, which was very strenuous and hard. Over a time, I became very tired and begged him to let me stop, but he pushed and pushed, his anger intensifying with every moment. Suddenly, I went into cardiac arrest and died.

This was not his intent, however, and over the years with Little Chinaman, he was able to let go of much his anger. The red in his aura signified his anger, and the yellow his intellectual, thus, physical realm perspective. Though he had no conscious desire for me to die, the event signified a spiritual death, a death he also suffered in our previous life.

After watching a few moments from above, I returned through the tunnel, back home.

THE GREAT TREE

Red Jacket channeled a very simple Indian poem, but one that I found to be beautiful:

I am like the great tree,
who, after bearing witness
to day and night for hundreds of years,
cries silently to the Great Spirit,
"Oh, I understand!
There is oneness between light and dark!"
The tree silently and peacefully dies. . .
making room for new life,
and becomes one with all that is.

GHOST REALITIES

Wondering about haunted houses, my husband asked me to explain my perception of ghosts. "Most ghosts," I explained, "are just trying to get someone's attention, but are perceived fearfully, because they are not always seen. More threatening incidents are often the result of the soul's perception of himself. For instance, most hauntings begin with small things, such as door rapping, objects moving, or doors opening and closing, but they progress into more serious activities including threats and violence. As soon as ghosts are perceived, they are feared. People speak of them as demonic or evil entities, and some will even have the house exorcised by a priest who believes the entity to be the devil himself! It should not be surprising that the soul, lost as he is, grabs on to these negative titles and says to himself, 'They think I am a demonic entity, that must be what I am!' Their actions then reflect their self-image. Ghosts of this type can become very disturbed, and they need to be sent back to the light."

That night, I took my subconscious astral husband to the White House and we partied with the ghosts. These ghosts were not lost souls, however, just party animals. Enjoying the thrill of creating unexplained phenomena, these entities seldom haunt the same place every night. Swaying on a large crystal chandelier, I got Andy in on the fun. As we flew about the house, he understood that these entities were no threat. A lot of "ghosts" are really our own spiritual guides trying to get our attention! After enjoying our flights, we re-entered our bodies.

INDIAN SUMMER

Exiting my body, the time tunnel lay waiting for me to enter. Flying through, I entered another body.

Crossing a river via a swinging bridge, I went to an Indian prison community (the same one I have described earlier), which consisted of a few small shacks surrounded by wooden fences. The shacks were made of stone with leaky grass roofs, and an armed guard watched the entrance to prevent the Indian's escape.

Bringing food to the prisoners, the guards let me pass without a word. A young and beautiful Indian girl met me at the gate and took me back to the newly-built prison shacks. The Indians had been moved to a more secure place to prevent their escape. Surrounded by gates, guards and a river, the townspeople felt pretty secure that the escapes would no longer occur.

Three Indian men lived in one of these huts. They called themselves brothers, but I knew they were not biologically related, as they were brothers in love. Many Indians were held prisoner, but a special bond existed between myself and these three brothers, as they were my closest friends and confidants. Red Jacket was one of these brothers, and the intensity of our love was evident. Five women lived in the shack next door, also becoming very good friends. All escaped, but one, who died during the winter.

Dropped into a later point in time, I was bringing a cart, which looked somewhat like a wheelbarrow, of food and blankets into the prison area.

Inside the hut, we removed everything from the cart and an Indian climbed in. Covering him with blankets and dirty clothes, I casually walked out of the camp with my cart, no questions asked. The guards felt I was a very compassionate woman by feeding the Indians and washing their clothes.

On my way out with the prisoner, I ran into my husband, who was entertaining three guests, two men, and one lady. For a moment, I felt that this would be a good opportunity to get him involved in the operation, but quickly realized it was not. Andy was trying to impress his guests with lavish gifts, as they were celebrating the men's recent graduation from some type of school. "Why don't you join us in our celebrating, honey?" he asked, as I looked down at my concealed prison escapee. I responded quickly, "In a moment. Let me put my cart in the house, and I will meet you at the general store." With that, he and his uppity guests waved and turned to leave. Bringing the Indian to an old log cabin, I hid him in a closet. Having been an old storefront, the cabin was nailed shut after going out of business. After we had created our own secret entrance in the back, I left the Indians there, and at nightfall, they would sneak out of the fort. I brought the cart to my home, and headed for the general store.

The general store was a log building near the center of town where many people went to socialize. Inside, the shop owner, a man of about 55 with gray hair, thin, and smoking a pipe, was catering to my husband, who was buying the most expensive cigars in the store for everyone there. A wooden counter with a very archaic version of a cash register stood at the left side of the store, while the right displayed a small selection of rifles for sale on the wall. Angered at my husband for wasting money on those who didn't need it, I tried to slip into the background. As the talk turned to the recent Indian escapes, I expressed my outrage and excused myself to leave.

Dropped into a further point in time, the escape drama continued. Red Jacket slipped into the cart, and I began the next escape operation. Taking him to the abandoned cabin, he climbed out of the cart and pulled me close to him. It had been quite some time, and we had fallen in love. Consummating our love, he asked me to come with him, "You are one of us, and do not belong here. Come with me and we will share our lives with each other. The Indian people will accept you and love you!" Tempted, I thought about it for a while, but I did not have the courage to make such a hasty decision. Night was upon us, and he had to leave while he could. "No, I love you very much, but I cannot leave, not yet, anyway." Smiling as he embraced me, he said, "I love you with all my heart." Moments later he was gone, and I would never see him again! Crying softly as he departed, I pulled myself together, as I knew I had to get home so as not to arouse suspicion.

Red Jacket pulled me out of the body and my vantage point was changed to watching from above. Andy was there, subconscious astral, watching the lifetime and getting angry. The case was clear-cut to him: I had an affair, so I was wrong.

Little Chinaman stepped in and said, "Your anger is an illusion, as love simply is. Red Jacket and your wife have a very deep spiritual bond, and it is beautiful. Your bond with her in that life was not the bond you share now. You and Marilynn share a very spiritual bond in this lifetime, and it is beautiful, too." Apparently, we all have many soul-mates, and when it comes right down to it, everyone is our soul-mate! Red Jacket represented a way of life that I admired, and my subconscious remembered my past lives as an Indian. He had that spiritual quality that I wanted to grasp, and Andy was in a different illusion.

ANOTHER LIFE TO LIVE

Cruising through the time tunnel, I was dropped into the body of a courtesan in what appeared to be the 17th century.

Lying in a field of grass wearing a beautiful pale blue gown,

the man I loved lay beside me. Wearing the traditional knick-
ers with stockings, black lace shoes, a vest, and a puffy shirt,
he was telling me of a small home he had bought for me. His
dark wavy hair and piercing green eyes made him irresistible
to me.

It was evident that the man was married, and I was his
mistress. Intending to "keep" me, he wanted to provide me
with all my needs. Strong-willed woman that I was, it angered
me that he had not consulted me in choosing a home, and I
did not feel that he respected my mind. I was very much in
love, however, and the affair continued for a short while
longer.

Before I moved into the house, though, a sudden and
unexplained break-up occurred. Maybe his wife had found
out about us and demanded it be stopped. Never hearing from
him again, I was heartbroken and didn't marry in that lifetime.

Dropped into a later time period, an old dying woman, I
passed over to the other side and wandered aimlessly for
several years. Ready to move on, an entity led me to a door
and told me to go through it. Inside my lover sat next to
another man that looked a bit like him. Many beings were in
the room, and they all appeared to be young. Floating in, I
tried to keep my hoop skirts quiet so as not to arouse any
attention, but they made no noise.

When I came into view, my lover turned and noticed me.
Flashing a big smile and sending thought-forms of love, he
drew me to him. Preoccupied, everyone was watching an
event on the earth-plane below. Turning to the man sitting
next to him, my lover introduced him as his son. "So you are
the woman my father loved so much!" he said. I sheepishly
smiled, acknowledging that it was mutual. A massive funeral
was going on in the earth-plane, and I was not sure what all
the fuss was about. Overflowing with pride, my lover chimed,
"My son, of whom I am very proud, was an important man!"
Waiting a moment to see if I would recognize him, he added,
"My son was Thomas Jefferson, third president of the United
States!" A beautifully-carved beige casket was being lowered
into the ground, the mourners crying. A voice behind me
explained that the man I loved could not have left his wife
without a scandal, and they had stayed together for
propriety's sake. He had loved me very much, and the love

was real. Taking my hand, we soared away. I was removed from the scene and relinquished to my physical body.

Thomas Jefferson died in 1826, so my lifetime occurred in that time period. Ironically, this same person had entered the present lifetime, and we met after I was married. Experiencing the same frustration as I had, as we could never be more than friends, his karma was balanced.

THE BULL

One evening, while standing in front of a mirror, a spirit channeled through. Pulling my hair up, it exclaimed, "Inside my head, rages the bull!" He immediately left my body. I was intrigued.

A few weeks later, I found that in the Indian medicine way, the term bull is used to identify the male buffalo, as well as, cows. The buffalo represents "a new understanding," and the spirit was commenting on my new understandings of reality. Inside my head rages a new understanding!

A problem with my child had cropped up involving spiritual entities in the home. For months, Melissa had played hours on end with her spiritual guides at night, laughing and talking. All of a sudden, she began to cry hysterically, as if someone was bothering her. Immediately, communication began.

There were two possibilities: she could be seeing a lost soul, or entities from a former lifetime could be making contact. In Melissa's case, it was the latter. When she cried, I went into trance, communicating to the spirits that they must leave her alone, as she was not ready to deal with them. Having no desire to traumatize her, they left immediately to return when she was older.

According to Indian wisdom, we must learn to see from all four directions of the medicine wheel which symbolize Wisdom, Innocence and Trust, Illumination, and Introspection. Allowing yourself to see through these directions, you will see that there is nothing to fear. These four qualities combined lead to seeing from the spiritual realm, thus real reality. If you are being plagued by a spirit, know that there are answers.

CHAPTER NINE
GRAY ROBE

MISSING IN ACTION

Passing through the vibrational state and the time tunnel, I was dropped into a lifetime during World War II. Living on an Indian reservation with my seven-year-old child, my mother was dead. My father, an aristocratic white, with gray wavy hair, a moustache curled with wax, black hat, coat, and cane, was making one of his infrequent visits to the reservation. Feeling nothing for the man, as he had not raised me, I paid little attention to his presence.

The reservation was located near a forest, and our small square homes were built around each other in a circular fashion. Every night, we would build a campfire and commune with one another. The father of my beautiful little girl was fighting in the Second World War, and I missed him greatly.

Filling up on supplies for the community at a military commissary, I looked up and noticed a familiar face. "Gray Robe! Is that you!" I shouted, running towards the Indian man. When he turned, I could not conceal my disappointment as he was not Gray Robe. Preparing me for some bad news, he somberly said, "Gray Robe has just been reported as missing in action." Crying softly, I was not surprised. "We were good friends," he said, "he was very brave and he loved you and your little girl very much." Carrying the supplies, he returned with me to the reservation.

In our camp circle that night, I was silent. Halfway through the evening, the man stood up and told of Gray Robe's status. The old Indian chief took me aside. An aging Indian with more patience than anyone I knew, he walked with me and explained the choices that Gray Robe had made. "Gray Robe was in a healing lifetime, as his aura was filled with the color green. Giving back to those he has taken from in the past, he chose

to move on. Hold his love within your heart and set him free."
Wanting to do that for him, I nodded in understanding. Gray
Robe was also Red Jacket. Giving his life to pay back for the
lives he had taken during the Indian wars, he was settling his
karma. As we sat on the ground, the Indian master raised his
hands to the sky and shouted to the heavens, "In our love, we
set you free, Gray Robe." A moment of introspection followed,
before I was pulled from the body.

STOCKPILE RESOLUTION

In a thought-form of a theatre, one of my unresolved stockpile friends appeared. It was empty, except for my friend who
occupied the first seat in the second row of chairs. A brilliant
red curtain completely closed off the stage, and behind it, you
could hear the sounds of a performance.

Sitting directly behind my friend, he turned and smiled.
"As the curtain conceals the illusion, I am ready to discard my
own." Recognizing him, I was very excited that this was
finally going to be resolved. "I understand your actions now,
and I am very glad that you are happily married and have a
beautiful child. I am at peace with it." Sending thought-forms
of love my way, it was over. Returning to my body, I felt very
loved.

THE RACE

In an astral thought-form, I joined several runners about to
begin a marathon race. I was determined to take a slow pace,
as the race was long, and the other runners quickly passed me
by. Happy with my pace, as I was perceiving everything along
the road, I could not help but wonder if I should speed up and
keep pace with the others. After a while, the other runners
sped by so quickly, I saw only a blur in their wake. Confused
about my role, I considered speeding up.

Suddenly, another runner pulled up alongside me going
my pace. Immediately sensing my thoughts, he replied, "The
other runners are caught up with the finish line, and you are
more interested in the path." Looking at him, I said, "But I feel
so separate and apart from their reality..." He interjected, "As
you should! You feel the oneness, and you see their reality for
what it is. They see it from a different illusion. To them,

physical life is all there is, winning is all there is. Spiritual growth requires a different perspective. One that you now have. Growth comes from within, not without. By taking life at the pace you have chosen, you allow yourself to perceive more accurately what the world truly represents. You embrace the divine plan and trust it completely, they do not. They feel that their importance lies in finishing the race with the fastest time, and you see that the race will never end. Every perception along the path is a crucial and important one. If you miss the flower on the side of the road because you ran by too quickly, you will need to return to perceive it in the future. In their ignorance, they may think they are passing you by, but the truth is, you have not even entered their race. Your path is parallel to their road, and they have not begun the path that you seek. The irony is that the race is an illusion. Do not compare yourself with those who see only illusion. Walk slowly down your path of increasing awareness and opening perceptions, as it is this path that leads to enlightenment."

Taking my hand, the entity and I went into a grocery store, and watched the illusion below. Listening to thoughts, and observing actions, we talked and compared perceptions. "Knowing what you know about the universe, would you choose to again become ignorant of it?" My response was a resounding no! He continued, "You may feel lonely and separate at times in your physical world because of your differing perceptions. But truth is a wonderful gift, and those who have truth, have everything.

Your loneliness is just another part of that illusion. Is it not true that we are always with you? Is it not true that we are available to you at all times? And, if this is so, then your loneliness is only a false perception on your part, as all who feel lonely perceive an illusion. You are never alone, it is an illusion!"

Suddenly realizing that this being must be a guide, I looked at him more closely. Manifesting as a twenty-ish man, with straight brown hair, a little pudgy and wearing contemporary clothing, he let my hand go and began floating off into the distance. From afar he called to me, "Remember, you have universal truth, you have oneness! How is it that you could ever be alone?!"

Feeling extremely loved and peaceful, I returned to my body and awoke.

DEATH OF AN OWL

In a thought-form reality out of my body, I saw an owl perched upon a fence in the middle of a dirty ghetto. His beauty was so immense, that I created a thought-form camera to take a picture of him. The beautiful bird began to fly, and moments later landed on my arm in a peaceful perch.

I stared at his majesty, and it surprised me when he began to wobble and look weak. Falling to the ground, the bird lay dying. Sadness overcame me, as I loved this bird, but I realized that it was the owl's time to move on and I must let him go. Spreading his wings, he turned to face the ground and died.

This was significant, as it represented a letting go of my single-vision. Born into the vision of the North, of wisdom, I had a need to incorporate the other three directions so that I might see things from a balanced perception. This owl represented that wisdom, and his death, the letting go and expansion of my perception.

Going through another vibration raising after a recent flu attack, I could not transmute the energy. My asthma would react, spurning the need for an intense inward search.

THREADBARE

Experiencing a past-life through an intense dream, I traveled to a point in time several hundred to a thousand years ago. My name was Thread Bear and my father was called Night Bear.

Our Indian camp split into three factions, due to three differing perceptions. Night Bear led a group that believed in war and strength; the man I loved led those who perceived through music; and I was the leader of a faction involved in birth. We were unable to meld our perceptions into one, and accept each other's realities.

Our camp was surrounded by pine trees and mountains, and several women were preparing to give birth. One clear, dark night, a woman in our camp went into labor. Just as the baby was born, a lightning-bolt struck a pine tree, despite the clear night sky. In honor of the child's exalted birth, we named her "Lighted Pine."

With the child's birth, we realized the stupidity of the

disagreement with our people. Summoning the other camp leaders, we joined together and called an end to the feud. Radiating love, a beautiful woman from the camp of music spoke to me. "Now we can share our music with you, our way of perceiving." Smiling, I replied, "I would love to hear your music. It is wonderful that Lighted Pine has opened us to perceiving in many ways." Looking a bit more serious, she said, "It is good that you want to hear our music, as it is all written by our leader, and they are all love songs written for you." Turning, she walked away leaving me in a state of wonder and love. Due to our different perceptions, I had turned away everyone, including the man I loved.

I left that beautiful lifetime behind, with all the camps were united together, and a beautiful pine glowed with the light of love in the middle of the community.

It is important to accept all ways of perceiving as one, as part of the same path.

THE DRIVE-BY

A presence became obvious, and I began to tune into the spirit's reality. A lost soul who suffered a traumatic death was in need of assistance.

A victim of a drug-related drive-by shooting, he showed me thought-forms of his death. About one hundred bodies were lying dead on the ground after a car drove by, with someone in it shooting a machine gun. Living through his initial wounds, he saw all of his friends die and fall to the ground. Moments later, he died, too. In reality, five or six people were killed, but lost souls often see things in an exaggerated fashion.

Understanding his fear, I said, "You sure must have suffered a lot seeing all of your friends die. It must be very painful to see such horror and then to be cut off from the world. But, you know, I love you a lot and I am going to help you find what you need." Feeling the love I sent to him, the entity put his hand on my face, lovingly. "Please don't do that," he said, "as it scares me. I haven't completely worked out all my fears." Backing off, he listened as I explained "reality" to him.

Afterwards the entity was calm, sending a thought-form of love and thanks. A cool breeze blew over me, and the being returned to God!

A SHARED EXPERIENCE

After asking Emmanuel to help me to understand the reasons for the manifestation of my asthma, I told him I was willing to face my fears head-on.

Leaving my body and heading through the tunnel, I dropped into the body of a brassy short-haired blonde wearing a red cocktail dress which appeared to be from the twenties. My husband at the time, who I knew to be Andy, was wearing a hat and a gray suit, which appeared to be from the same time frame.

We were at a big party with about one hundred people attending. The party was held in a huge, red-brick mansion with white pillars and a circular driveway. Parked in front of the house were two model-T cars.

From behind, someone grabbed me, a gun to my back, and dragged me to an empty room. Shots were heard from the other room, and two men beat me and shot me in the chest three times. After such commotion, the heat was on, and they rushed out of the room.

I was still alive, and the paramedics put me on a stretcher and carted me outside to the waiting ambulance. Going through the main room of the house, the coroner was leaning over my dead husband's body. All the guests watched anxiously as we were removed from the home.

In my hospital room, ready to die, I tried phoning the police to tell them who my attackers were. But I lost consciousness and died quickly, and no one would ever know it was a mob hit.

When I returned to my body, I still felt the pain from the gunshots. Waking up, my husband asked me what was wrong. When I told him, he looked at me strangely, and replied, "I just had the exact same dream!"

NEW YORK

While taking a nap during the afternoon, I underwent a vibrational raising. Leaving my body, I flew about the room, and turned off the TV. At the window, I watched the mailman deliver our mail, and enjoying the freedom of my astral body,

I flew up, down, and all around. Venturing further, I went to an apartment in New York City.

In a high-rise apartment building, I flew to one of the top floors and looked around. The familiarity of the place intrigued me, as I knew that I had been here before. Four doors were in the hallway, an elevator, and a beautiful staircase with golden handle-rails. A man walked out one of the doors, and I felt recognition. Moments later, a female walked out a different door, and I realized that this was another part of me living in another reality of this time period!

Following her, she was on her way to a dumpy bar on the wrong side of town. I watched her for about an hour, while she sang in a rock band that worked at the club. Then she went back to her "dressing room," which was nothing more than an old utility closet. After finishing up, she walked down the streets admiring the graffiti smeared on every building. I left the scene to return home.

In the vibration state, Emmanuel put his hands on my stomach and sent warm energy through my being. As I returned to consciousness, he put his arm around me and gave me a hug!

A POEM FOR MOM

With a little help from Red Jacket, I wrote a poem for my mother who does not understand my spiritual journey. I dedicate this to her with love. . .

THE TWIN TREES

Two trees stand tall in the woods,
one a birch and one a pine.
The pine tree is taller,
to show the effect of time.

The birch tree looks up to the pine,
and turns to call her "Mom."
She says, "I love you very much,
but I must sing my own song!"

"I want to grow up towards the sky,
and see the flocks of birds!

I want to grow above the woods,
and see the prairie herds!"

The pine responds lovingly,
"Go, pursue your dreams.
But don't get struck by lightning,
like all the tallest trees!"

"Growing tall may be it for you,
but me, I'll stay right here.
I am safe beneath the tallest pines,
but do what you must, my dear."

The birch grew taller over the years,
she grew towards the sky.
She saw the prairie herds, afar,
and she watched many birds fly by.

One day she looked down towards her mom,
buried underneath the trees.
"Oh, Mother Pine, I love you so,
and I have learned to be."

"It's time for me to move along,
I've grown, so, as a tree.
Tomorrow, I will end my stay,
as there is so much for me to see!"

A storm was brewing the very next day,
and the birch was not surprised.
A lightning bolt hit her branch,
and the birch tree quietly died.

The mother pine cried softly,
as she could not understand.
When suddenly she felt a touch,
on her branch she felt a hand!

She looked below her branches,
to find the source of the touch.
A human being sat next to her,
eating a bagged lunch.

The woman looked up at the pine,
and smiled the biggest smile.
"It's good to see you, mommy,
it has been quite a while!"

"It could not be,"
the pine tree thought,
"My little girl is dead."
But doubt crept away, light shone in her eyes,
and knowing came instead!

The tears flowed long from the pine trees eyes,
but the pine tree was not sad.
She spread her branches and began to grow,
through the forest roof above her head.

The pine grew tall over the years.
She grew towards the sky!
She saw the prairie herds, afar,
and she saw the birds fly high!

Then one day, the clouds came in,
and a storm began to brew.
The pine was struck by lightning,
her eternal life ensued!

She looked down from the heavens,
to find her little girl,
her daughter appeared beside her,
in a cloud-like whirl.

They smiled at each other,
as they understood the divine plan.
"Come on, mom," said the daughter,
and they went to earth as man!

THE FACE IN THE WINDOW

Enjoying the peace of the vibrational state, I prepared to
leave my body. Entering into a different dimension which

almost looked like a "Flintstones" reality with stone slab houses, I lay comfortably on a slab of rock inside a home.

Resting peacefully and enjoying the connection to the God-mind, my guide came to a window right above where I lay and spoke. This was the guide who helped me to understand the importance of my own truth in my illusory racetrack of life.

Showing me thought-forms of my fears and conflicts, he said, "In order to understand true reality behind your earthly conflicts, you must see the window of perception that other beings see through." Showing me more thought-forms of my mother's perception, and of other people in my life, he smiled. "Allow yourself to tune into others' perceptions, so that you may understand the parameters of their vision. If you allow that spiritual reality, you will understand these conflicts to be unnecessary and illusory. Love all beings, despite their present manifestation, as love is the only reality."

Thanking him for his wise words, I waved good-bye, and journeyed back to my body.

CHAPTER TEN

AND YOU WILL BE MY TEACHER. . .

THE OLD MAN

In the astral state, I entered into a large, all-white mansion which stood in a clearing in the woods. A familiar family was there, subconscious astral, and they treated me with great respect. Asking questions about my experiences, we talked for a short while. When finished, they led me to a very large room which was all white and completely empty, except for a little old man sitting in a folding chair at the far corner of the room. As he motioned me forward, they closed the door and left.

Looking up at me with his tired eyes, suspenders and worn-out clothing, he replied very calmly, "And you will be my teacher." Confused, I responded, "But there are so many teachers. . . ." He interrupted, saying again, "And you will be my teacher."

Frustrated, I asked, "But what will I teach you?" He looked up, and books appeared all over the room, each one a different metaphysical topic all with the same theme of unconditional love. Browsing, I looked at the books. A spirit voice was heard from above, "You don't need these books, as it is all within your heart!" As I put the books down, the old man repeated, "And you will be my teacher." He paused a moment, and then continued. "I am an old foolish man, and I represent a very old and foolish society, and you will teach me!" Bowing to the old man, I nodded in agreement. As I turned to leave, every thing disintegrated into mid-air, and I went home.

Upon my return, I began to recall vividly a vision I had had as a child. Knowing it to be important at the time, I had remembered it always. This event had spurred it's recall.

As I stood between realms of existence in my etheric body, the clouds began to whirl and heave as the heavens opened up. A beautiful entity whom I perceived as God or Jesus, sat in a golden throne, with marble steps leading to this wondrous being. Angelic beings were flying all around, and I was motioned to come forth.

A vision was presented to me of the cross burning, and myself trying to put it out. My family could not see the cross, only the fire, and we battled over this differing perception. In the end, I put the fire out and the cross stood tall.

The powerful being spoke: "The fire represents ignorance, and the cross, awareness. There will be much fire in your family, but you will bear the cross. As they will never see it, you may find frustration. At a future time, you will take that cross to the world and present it as a living vision of the reality of God. Though others may think you are foolish, you are special. All mankind will learn of the cross, and see their own divinity. Be patient, and let it be."

With that, thunder struck and the heavens began to close. Filled with love, I was changed forever. The vision never left me, and now its feeling was renewed.

As we are all important in the second coming of the Christ Consciousness, we should all pay heed to this message. Thousands of people like me and you are scattered about the world to become living examples of love and light for others to see. Small sparks of remembrance lead others to begin their own inward journey, and each of us has our own special purpose in that plan.

NEW PERCEPTIONS

In a dream, my husband and I were on a wooded mountain overlooking a large city. Balloons were flying by, the sounds of a crowd were heard from a stadium nearby, and I felt a strong urge to be free. Contemplating in my mind, I thought of how nice it would be to be single and childless.

In a radical change, the city disappeared, and my husband bent over, picking up roots and herbs. Alone on the mountain, he looked at me with his beautiful smile, and I saw a different person. My eyes were seeing him for the first time, yet, I saw everything I knew of him, also. Feeling extremely lucky, I reveled in the wonderful relationship we had, and our beautiful lives together.

The lesson in this experience was that older relationships only appear less exciting because we alter the perception in which we view our partners. If you allow yourself to see through the original eyes you saw each other, the love and excitement returns.

EMMANUEL'S LAUNDRY

While I was washing my dishes in the kitchen, the clothes dryer turned itself on. Intrigued, as I had already done all the laundry for the day, I checked the dryer to find it empty and set to go for 75 minutes. Laughing, I knew that Emmanuel was summoning me into his realms.

Cruising out of body, I found myself in a very large cavern. Feeling so comfortable and at home, I forgot I was traveling astrally, and paid little attention to what was happening or the entity I was following. Flying about through the cavernous dens and up a set of stone steps, I thought, "Oh, shoot, I am out of my body, I should be paying closer attention to this." I looked around, trying to remember what this place meant to me and what I was supposed to learn. Hopelessly lost, the entity I had been following was gone and I returned to my body.

Emmanuel wanted me to bring more conscious involvement into my astral experiences. Basking in the familiarity of the situation, I was not bringing everything back.

THE ISLAND OF TRUTH

While I was in a thought-form reality, my guides taught me a lesson about the attainment of truth.

In a schoolroom, I and about twenty students were preparing to take a test. The space I inhabited looked very foggy to me, and I wouldn't understand why until later.

The teacher, a young, balding, thin man of average height, was giving us a test on truth. Almost like a spelling test, he would tell us his truth, and we had to write it down exactly as he said it. Trouble was, he spoke so fast that no one could possibly keep up with him. Getting three out of the ten right, I went to the teacher and asked for another chance, as I truly wanted to understand.

His desk was sitting on the bank of a muck pond which had an island in the middle. Ten stone pillars could be seen clearly from the bank, and according to the teacher, the truths were etched in the stone. "Only I know what these pillars say, and because of that, no one will ever pass this test. The answers are on that island, but do not try to jump across, as many have tried and never returned!" Confused, I agreed not to go.

Another group of students came in, all failing his test. Having paid closer attention, I realized that his words were not difficult to understand, but the teacher meant something different than what was heard. He was tricking them!

Realizing that I did not have to jump across the muck pond, I willed my etheric body to the island of truth. There was no fog. Looking down on the pillars for their ominous message, I found pastries, instead. Understanding came, and the teacher's fraud became clear. His truths were not on this island, as he had never been there. Truths are not etched in stone, because they are constantly changing. The message in the pastries was of simplicity and fun.

Many entities were enjoying themselves on the island, and I understood them to be these souls who had "never made it to the island." They had found truth, and did not need to return. In his fear, the teacher never perceived them on the island, though they stood right in front of his eyes. In his arrogance, he saw only danger. The real truth was that the man on the bank was afraid to step into awareness, as he was afraid of the unknown.

Perpetuating his own fear, he told the other entities seeking truth that only he had it, and that it was too dangerous for them to find it themselves. A few brave souls, however, decided that they must find truth for themselves.

The message in this beautiful experience was to never give your power to the man on the bank (a church, or any person), as truth is your destiny to find!

FULFILLING MY PURPOSE

The work with lost souls had become draining on me, and I asked Emmanuel to give me a break. Understanding my discomfort, he agreed.

After a two-week vacation, he took me to see the book of records, which contains all the information about every entity, past, present, and future, and most importantly, the purpose of each lifetime.

We entered a dimension of light, and it seemed that everything and everyone was just glowing with white light! Passing a series of rooms through the hallways of light, we entered into a book-filled space. Emmanuel telepathically asked the librarian-entity for the material he needed, and the being flew to the ceiling, picked out a glowing white book, and let it float to Emmanuel's hands.

The listings looked a bit like want ads, and he found my name. Covering four of the five listings under my name, he allowed me to see only one. "Being in the physical realm to aid in the journey of lost souls." Clearly, this was one job I could not quit. I asked Emmanuel to help me with my fears and anxieties about lost souls, and I promised that I would fulfill that purpose! I returned to my body and awoke.

CHAKRA CONTROL

After a long discussion with Red Jacket and Emmanuel, I felt more at ease about the lost soul task. Knowing that they were going to help me, the next lost soul would not be so draining. The most traumatic part of dealing with these souls was seeing their horrible deaths replayed, as they were all very violent and gory. Emmanuel was working on a new partnership that would be easier for me, but just as effective. I would be introduced to his new plan in a few weeks. In the meantime, Emmanuel had other plans for me.

In a conscious sleep-state, Emmanuel spoke with me about entering the vibrational state on my own. "You must psychically transplant your chakra energy into your third eye or sixth chakra." Doing as he said, I immediately went into the vibrational state. Leaving my body, I hovered in another room of the house watching Andy and Melissa. Andy looked up and his subconscious responded, "Oh, there you are!" Returning to my body, Emmanuel had me do this several times. The vibrational force was not as steady as when they did it, but after several practice tries, I accomplished it with little effort.

Emmanuel left me with a short channeled message:

"Those who do not seek awareness, do not seek it because a part of them knows they will find something they cannot turn away from. This something will make them different, and they will no longer feel a part of their illusory world. This, my friends, is more frightening than any horror imaginable! But these who do seek, find that there is much joy in truth. Many beings are arrogant in their ignorance, as those who know the least profess the most. Awareness brings the knowing that there is no limit to the divine plan!"

THE CHANT

In a channeling space bordering on another dimension, a gregorian chanter began a soulful eastern melody:

I am the grandfather, old and wise.
I know the answers you just can't deny.
But you have not found me, yet.
But you have not found me, yet.

Swept into the beauty of his song, he repeated it over and over again. A glowing shrine of jewels appeared before my eyes, and an old, old man with long white hair and a beard sat. His legs were crossed and his eyes closed. Wearing a white robe with hands placed on his knees, he phased in and out of the dimension I occupied. Very moved by the peaceful music, I flowed with its simple rhythm.

Upon my return, I knew that this entity was very important to me, and I needed to contact him. At a later point in time, I would.

AN EMMANUEL SESSION

EMMANUEL: (laughing) Hello.

ANDY: Hi Emmanuel, sure am glad you are with us, again!

EMMANUEL: It's nice to be back.

ANDY: It really has been too long since we last talked.

EMMANUEL: Yes, it gets more difficult to come through.

ANDY: Why is that?

EMMANUEL: With frequency, our atoms mesh better.

ANDY: Marilynn wanted to know, in regards to her book, is there a purpose she should be focusing on, like publication?

EMMANUEL: The most important thing at this time is documentation. She should pursue publication, but not look at publication as a means to an end. The path of writing these things helps her to grow. We will take care of publication on our end. She just needs to submit the book to publishers. It will happen when it is time.

ANDY: Another question is that she seems to have such a strong desire to evolve, whereas, I am sincere but have not given it such a high priority. Do you have any thoughts on that?

EMMANUEL: You have learned to be, and she has not.

ANDY: I find that a surprising answer, I thought it was the other way around.

EMMANUEL: (laughing) Sometimes, appearances can be deceiving.

ANDY: I feel so much love from you when we talk.

EMMANUEL: You are greatly loved.

ANDY: I have felt you a few times recently in the house.

EMMANUEL: I am here very often.

ANDY: I'd like to ask you about a couple of interesting dreams. One, I was scratching a window, and Marilynn was very scared. I looked through the window and saw the face of a dark-haired woman who seemed very peaceful. Marilynn didn't want me to see her, and when I did, I got scared. She turned and walked away. Any thoughts?

EMMANUEL: Perhaps if she was wise enough to walk away, you should let it be. You must pursue this with her personally, as she is with you.

ANDY: Okay, the other thing: I dreamed I was in a basement. A man and a woman appeared and seemed to be floating by. Shortly thereafter, a heavyset man came in and sat on me, and he had something coming out of his stomach. The other entities came towards me and I became scared. I told them to leave, and they left.

EMMANUEL: Sometimes your wife is wiser than you may think. (laughter) Your guides appeared to you, two of them, whom you recognized as such. Then, you feared, and distorted them in your mind, creating monsters.

I have been given permission by a certain entity to give you more. (laughter) The dark-haired woman is a spiritual friend, someone you have known for a long time, and your wife fears her, as she perceives her to be a threat.

ANDY: Thank you, and she is smart sometimes!

EMMANUEL: Pursue this!

ANDY: If I am already "being," why should I devote more energy and time to reading?

EMMANUEL: Your wife has been through many lifetimes, and her constant hurdle is the desire to do something of great importance. As you have learned to be, you can help her to become satisfied with who she is, not what she represents. This is a greater goal than any title or accomplishment.

When I say you have learned to be, it does not mean there is no room for growth. Inward growth is where your wife excels, and this is what she will teach you. She is very adept at traveling amongst the realms, and you have great fear of that. So, as you can see, it all balances out quite well.

What an illustrious game! (laughter)

ANDY: It helps to focus on it as a game.

EMMANUEL: As it is.

ANDY: It helps me at work to take it less seriously. (Andy is a prosecuting attorney.)

EMMANUEL: A game you play a role in. However, do not feel responsible for the growth of every being that enters your courtroom. That is their own journey.

ANDY: We have been having a lot of trouble with Melissa since she's been born, especially Marilynn. We have tried to figure out her sudden outbursts of screaming when confronted with simple situations.

EMMANUEL: A suggestion that I will give rather lightly is, when she decides to cry out exasperatingly, you must perceive it as an intriguing move in a very intriguing game (laughing). Your wife is beginning to understand, though it is hard for her to accept, that certain aspects of this child are very normal. She certainly is a difficult child, but there are reasons for everything aren't there! Your wife is evolving rather rapidly as a result of this, and if this is any consolation, she has told me many times that her ultimate goal is growth. So, (laughing) it's happening.

ANDY: I hope we will survive!

EMMANUEL: Oh, we will all survive. Your wife has the presence of mind to know of her own weaknesses. Many people are not willing to recognize their twin nature. Through great trial and tribulation, your wife has been able to resolve that many of her problems with the child are related to herself. You have probably noticed that your wife is growing to a more whole and loving being.

It is all a game, and we will all win. Along the way, Marilynn will grow tremendously, and because of that, Melissa will also benefit. She needs it because of the trauma she suffered in Vietnam. With her return to earth, Melissa made a careful selection, as she wanted to grow in this lifetime. Because both of you have the courage to face the issues and learn, you will work through that anger and be able to treat each other in more loving ways.

ANDY: Can you tell us what happened to her in Vietnam?

EMMANUEL: Give me a few moments to access. . .(breathing loudly) She suffered a great deal. As you know, she was a man in that life and someone she loved greatly blew up before her eyes. Someone she might have married. . . There is great sadness as she is crying over the body, or what is left of it. It would not be beneficial to go into this further.

ANDY: Both of us had a dream, Marilynn a past-life experience, that somehow involved the mob. Could you comment on that.

EMMANUEL: It was a past life.

ANDY: I have always felt a strong connection. . .

EMMANUEL: With the twenties and thirties. You were there and so was she.

ANDY: Did we know each other?

EMMANUEL: Yes, but not for long, as you both were killed. You died very young.

ANDY: Both of us?

EMMANUEL: You died together.

ANDY: Can you tell us anymore, like who killed us?

EMMANUEL: A separate mob family. In a surprise attack, you were both shot.

ANDY: Were we members of a mob family?

EMMANUEL: You were, but your wife wasn't. The marriage to you brought her into the family.

ANDY: Could you tell us why Melissa chose to experience all this sadness and suffering in her past life?

EMMANUEL: She needs to learn to confront, as this has been a problem for her all her lives. Vietnam was a very extreme environment.

ANDY: What do you mean by learning to confront?

EMMANUEL: She has always been a conformist and cannot go against consensus reality. Like many of us, she wants to be accepted.

ANDY: I feel like my father really suffers from that, and I do, too.

EMMANUEL: It's very common. However, it is important

to accept your own self for what you are. Before you accept yourself, you never truly accept others.

ANDY: I seem to shun away from telling others about my growth in the spiritual plane.

EMMANUEL: It is your fear of not being accepted. In order to grow, you must let that go. Accepting that in your growth, you will leave others behind. Until you realize that your growth is more important than acceptance, you will stagnate. Telling others will light a spark of remembrance that may or may not be followed up. Just as others express their Christianity or other religion as their way of life, you should express your truths as part of you. Do not hide your reality, as hiding inhibits.

ANDY: I guess that is one way to grow. Any other suggestions?

EMMANUEL: Desire, and meditation. Marilynn really feels the desire and you do not.

You must take initiative, and it will grow. Marilynn has a tremendous capacity to feel and sense. As she senses the reality behind situations, she knows what people really feel and think, despite what their words say. You two conflict sometimes because she senses your truth, regardless of whether you are being honest with yourself. Because of this ability, it is more difficult to remain detached about situations. She feels very intensely, and she can feel another's pain as if it were her own. This sensitivity comes with a true feeling of oneness, as she can identify herself as part of every being.

Flow with your own being and desire to grow from your heart. As Marilynn is emotionally centered, and you intellectually, your approach to growth and understanding may be different. The emotional person finds the intellectual too grounded, and the intellectual finds the emotional too flaky.

ANDY: Marilynn has felt that maybe she needs to communicate with other metaphysical people in order to grow.

EMMANUEL: Growth is individual and occurs when one basks in solitude. Marilynn must learn to discern between her truth and other beings' truths. She has a strong desire to help others due to her sensitivity, as she senses the pain and wants to relieve it. A small part of her has not let go of the illusion, and she must, as these beings need this for their growth.

ANDY: Ever since I was a child, my mother has spoken of

her brother, Andy, who died in World War II. I'd just like to know where he is.

EMMANUEL: He is quite happy, as he is a being of light. Andy is with us now.

ANDY: I wish I could tell my mother.

EMMANUEL: You can tell her. She may think you are nutty, but even she will pass onto the other realms and find truth someday. (laughing) He is expressing his regrets that his sister was so unable to let go of his memory, for he was very happy when he left and it was his time to move on. (pause) He is leaving and returning to the light.

ANDY: Marilynn wanted to know about Red Jacket's involvement with her at this time.

EMMANUEL: Red Jacket is a very good friend, but he is also leading her curriculum. (laughter) Marilynn has a vast Indian background, and Red Jacket is preparing her to meet her Indian master, who will be her next teacher when I am through.

She met this master once, but it will take a bit of time as he exists in a very high plane. It is essential for her to undergo many vibrational raisings and other preparation in order to meet him in such a high vibrational zone. He carries such an overwhelming amount of light!

ANDY: What do we on the planet earth have in store for us in the future? Will we destroy ourselves?

EMMANUEL: It depends on your perception of destruction. Nuclear annihilation will not occur, but there could be ecological destruction. Mother earth will never be completely destroyed by man, as the earth will decide when she is ready to return to God and complete the cycle herself. Consensus consciousness is not good at this time, and a lot of tragedies that occur are a result of that.

ANDY: I certainly agree with that. It seems more and more of our world leaders are becoming more greedy and selfish.

EMMANUEL: Most world leaders are inherently young souls, as they are the ones who require the power, ambition, and fame due to their over-developed egos.

ANDY: Should Marilynn continue to channel you, and are you the same entity who works with Pat Rodegast who wrote *Emmanuel's Book*?"

EMMANUEL: Yes, I am. I have worked with many beings

throughout time, and for selfish reasons, yes, I would like Marilynn to allow me to channel through her. (laughing)

ANDY: Why did Marilynn choose to have the health problems she is presently experiencing?

EMMANUEL: Most disease comes as a result of a denial of love, the fear of being loved totally. Some do it because they are ready to move on. Marilynn feels too responsible for other people, and she needs to learn to be. There is a positive aspect to her illness, as it has forced her to be introspective and spurred her communication with us in the spiritual realm. She sometimes thinks that because she is tired so much, that something is wrong. However, we are just bringing her into our realms to communicate and teach her.

ANDY: Marilynn would like to know how to open up more.

EMMANUEL: (laughing) We are connected with Marilynn all the time. She doesn't trust her own instincts enough. Take a chance and say, "You are saying this, but I am feeling this." She is afraid of appearing arrogant. Tell her to allow the openness that she already has, to become a part of her entire being.

I believe I must go now, as Marilynn has to go.

ANDY: Thanks for coming.

An intense session, my legs were dripping with sweat when I returned. All the entities that came in probably stirred up a lot of heat!

THE ITINERARY

Traveling out of my body, I ran across an Indian, very tall, dark and muscular, who took me to a forest.

The forest was displaying the splendor of summer with its full green carpet and flowers in bloom. An easel stood in a small clearing with an old parchment attached. The Indian pointed to the parchment and spoke, "This is a map of your spiritual growth in this lifetime." Pointing to a spot near the top of the map he continued, "As you can see, these are the next few steps you will take before meeting your Indian master." Pointing downward on the map, he said, "And this is what you have mapped for the rest of this lifetime, and down here in the corner is the day you have chosen to leave this earth." Understanding that the time was near for me to meet my Indian teacher, I returned to my body and awoke with no memory of the contents of the map.

Very soon after, I was asked by a local group to channel Emmanuel for them, but I was afraid. I had a dream that night, convincing me that I should.

Searching through the dirty attic of an old home, I came across a beautiful box hidden underneath the junk. Covered in gemstones of all colors, it shimmered in the light.

Opening the box, I found slips of paper naming cities and destinations, the first one reading "New Mexico to Valla Halla." As there were hundreds of slips, I sifted through them to the bottom of the box. A black and white photograph of me channeling for a group of people lay on the side. A spiritual voice was heard from above, "And you will be my teacher." Remembering my meeting with the old man, I felt an urgent need to return the box to where I had found it. Feeling as though I was disturbing a future truth, I placed the box under the pile of junk. Feeling a confirmation that I should channel for the group, I returned to my body.

CHAPTER ELEVEN
THE AGE OF AQUARIUS

BIG BLOCKS

Cruising into the vibrational state, I prepared to leave my body. Worry interfered as I thought of my child waking from her nap. Having lowered the vibrations a bit, I focused to bring them back up. Intervening again, I thought I heard the baby crying and my husband fluttering the newspaper. For a moment, I even worried that my body was not in a good position to leave. Trying to ignore my creations, it was too late, and the vibrations ceased.

Knowing that I had to let go of all my illusions to freely fly about, I put my trust in the divine plan. If I chose not to let go, transcending the physical illusion would not be possible. My worries had taken up all my mind space, and there was no room left. I quickly emptied my mind, by placing my worries in the hands of God.

THE AQUARIAN

In an astral thought-form, I was working with a spiritual theatre group playing many different parts. Trying every possible role, I could not find one that was right for me. The directing entity, a being manifesting as a middle-aged, balding man of less than average height, asked me to return for the next play.

Willing myself away, I found myself in a beautiful astral crystal shop. Shimmering white crystals covered the ceilings, walls, and floor, and I sat in a corner soaking up the intense vibrations. All the crystals were huge, like stalactites that form in caverns, and their energy pulsated my being for several minutes.

Knowing it was time to return to the theatre group, I willed myself back. The stage was filled with dancers, as they performed a drama about human nature. Two beings watched from their tables in the restaurant below the stage, and the actors were disappointed at the small showing. When I entered the backstage area, the director ran to me holding a white, flowing costume, "It is the age of Aquarius, and you are the Aquarian! You must play this part as it comes natural to you!" Recognizing my role, I smiled and took the costume. Everyone in the theatre group was excited, as this was the play we had been waiting for, and its time had come. Returning to my body, I awoke.

This thought-form represented the coming of the Age of Aquarius, the New Age, and my role as an Aquarian was to help bring in that New Age. The small audience represented the disappearance of the personal drama, and the onslaught of reality. Our new play, The New Age, would be performed to a full house!

Undergoing an intense vibration-raising a few days later, I felt like I was going up and down a thirty-story elevator very rapidly. As it was part of my preparation to meet my Indian master, I did not mind.

DEATH BY AN OUTLAW

Traveling through the time tunnel, I entered into the body of a western woman living on a prairie ranch. I had light brown hair and wore a blue, flower-print dress with a matching bonnet. A thin, small man with long, black, wavy hair stood next to me. He was my husband. He wore a weathered cowboy hat, and brown leather pants and a vest. Our two children were inside, a 4-year-old little girl with long blonde hair, and a 2-year-old boy with dark brown hair in a bobby cut.

My husband and I were walking away from our small three-room cabin with a pillared porch. Two farm hands were working with the animals and we walked toward them. Galloping horses were heard in the distance, and before we could look up and respond, gunfire rang out on our peaceful ranch. Three outlaws sped through our home, killing the two workmen and myself.

Watching from above, my husband was walking away from a freshly dug grave. One child on each side, I felt I could move on. Feeling certain that he would take good care of our kids, I sent them thought-forms of love and sped towards the light.

DIFFERING PERCEPTIONS

Returning to the house that once contained the box of future truth, I noticed a familiarity.

The home was old, run-down and completely different than the home we lived in, but I knew it occupied the same space. Looking through another window of perception, the house that I considered beautiful was not only ugly, but frightening. I heard a knock on the door, and a thought-form of Andy went to answer it amidst my protests.

This could be a fearful perception, as there are many ways to perceive the same thing. Or, this could be another home that occupied the same space a few hundred years before. Exiting the fear, the home returned to its familiar state.

Just as a person who has lived in the streets would perceive a two-bedroom house as a castle, that same home would be viewed as a dump by a person living in a 15-room mansion. There are many windows of perception in all things.

Hovering and flying about the city, I looked up and saw a friend who had met me earlier to work out a stockpile problem. Subconscious astral, he was flying about in a frenzy of joy, as his wife had just given birth to a baby. Flying with him to celebrate his new child, I took him to the clouds and we flew through them.

Leaving my friend behind, I flew about until I reached a large hospital. An old man lay in a bed preparing to die. Moments later, his monitors went blank and he exited his body. Overjoyed at what he saw, he reached out to his guides, and they grabbed his hand in an explosion of light! Intense excitement filled the being as they took him back to God.

Feeling peaceful and content, I returned to my body.

EMMANUEL'S DEBUT

Speaking with a group of about fifteen people, Emmanuel came through with his loving being.

EMMANUEL: Hello.
GROUP: Hello, is this Emmanuel?
EMMANUEL: Yes, it is.

QUESTION: Emmanuel, can you tell us where you are from?

EMMANUEL: I am from everyplace, and no-place. I am here and I am there. I can exist in all realities.

QUESTION: Have you ever been physical?

EMMANUEL: Yes, I have.

QUESTION: Was it on the earth-plane?

EMMANUEL: Yes.

QUESTION: Did you go through regular incarnations that we go through, or did you experience earth one time?

EMMANUEL: I experienced earth like all of you, it took me a bit of time.

QUESTION: Emmanuel, I would really like to open up more to channeling and communication with my guides. Could you give me suggestions as to what might help me open up?

EMMANUEL: There is fear that you are not aware of which blocks you. Your guides love you very much and desire to communicate with you. Ask them to help you identify your fears, so you may work through them.

QUESTIONER: Thank you.

EMMANUEL: You're welcome.

QUESTION: How can I achieve the things I want to achieve, and how am I blocking the achievements that I desire?

EMMANUEL: The question I would ask you, is what do you desire to achieve?

QUESTIONER: There are many things, and it is hard to pinpoint just one.

EMMANUEL: Are these physical, or spiritual?

QUESTIONER: Both. How about spiritual.

EMMANUEL: May I ask you what spiritual things would you like to achieve? In the now, at this point in time.

QUESTIONER: At this point, I would like to be in the now at all times.

EMMANUEL: Then the question answers itself. If you want to achieve all your desires, you must truly experience the now at all times. Allow yourself to enjoy the absence of pressure to reach the end of your path. Perceive everything along your path and you will realize that the finish line is not your goal. It is the path. Desire it, and it will happen.

QUESTIONER: Thank you.

EMMANUEL: You're welcome.

QUESTION: I would like to ask what drew me here tonight. I did not want to come, but something made me feel as if I should. When I met Marilynn, I felt a strong connection.

EMMANUEL: (Laughing) There are no coincidences, you know. You and Marilynn have met in a previous life; explore it. May I say that you were brothers.

QUESTIONER: But I like my brother in this life.

EMMANUEL: (Laughing) Give Marilynn a chance. (Group laughing) In terms of what you were drawn here for, Marilynn has a lot of experience on the astral plane, we have dragged her through the mud, shall I say! (Laughing) You have a desire to experience that, and she can help you.

QUESTION: What was Jesus Christ's message, and how and why was it distorted?

EMMANUEL: Jesus's real message was that all the knowledge of the universe is within each and every one of us. It was distorted because of fear. People wanted to create a persona of a being greater than they, and that was an illusion, as he is one with us. Jesus Christ came to help you unleash all that you are within your own being.

QUESTION: I would like to know how I can make a better connection in my channeling, how am I blocking it?

EMMANUEL: Doubt. If you doubt their existence, it is more difficult for them to come in. Embrace them with your energy, so they may embrace you with theirs. Do not feel unworthy of this connection with higher teachers, release the doubt.

QUESTION: I feel as though I am between worlds, and am going through a transition. I feel kind of strange and detached at times. I feel like I should be doing something.

EMMANUEL: (Laughing) Excuse me for laughing as you sound very much like my student, Marilynn, who had trouble with being.

You are between worlds, you are between truth and blindness and the transition can be very difficult. Truth, however, is the greatest gift of all and if you had the choice to turn back and become a part of the illusory world, you would not choose that. And so the path must continue.

At this point, you need to experience the now and embrace the oneness. There are things in store for you in the future, but in the now you must grow. Allow yourself the time to grow and discover your purpose with your own guides. Journey inward, as all the answers lie within you.

QUESTION: I would like to know why my birth was so traumatic?

EMMANUEL: Trauma is an illusion. Experiencing birth is experiencing confinement—leaving a world where thoughts are things, flight and fancy are a way of life, and entering a newborn body that cannot even move on its own. It is not unusual for some to struggle and have a change of heart.

QUESTION: I find that I am very skeptical about things. Can I use this as a tool in my growth?

EMMANUEL: Skepticism is a way of discerning, which is very important, as there are many windows of perception. Even in the spiritual planes, we perceive through different windows. Each truth is real and valid. Skepticism is okay, but discernment is the goal. Find what is truth for you and embrace it.

QUESTION: I, too, feel like I am going from one plane of existence to another, and I need to let go of the past and move into the future. I have fears of what might be in the future, because of the unknowing. I agree with living in the now, but is there more?

EMMANUEL: Part of growth is accepting the divine plan. Part of accepting the future is knowing that whatever happens will be right. Those in transition want the book opened for them, but the goal of enlightenment is to open the book yourself. The future is entirely up to you. It would be unfair of me, or anyone, to tell you exactly what to expect from your future as that would take away your free will. We all create our own reality, and though it would be nice to have someone tell us what to do, that would only inhibit growth. You would no longer need to pursue your own inward journey.

Let go of the past and experience being-ness. Being is a state of ultimate happiness and fulfillment in the state that you are now. It is the state when you no longer look forward and say, "This is the day I will be happy." Rather, "I am happy now, I will be happy tomorrow, and whatever comes is part of the divine plan. I have a choice in what I create!"

QUESTION: Are there any goals I should be pursuing, or should I just live day to day? Should I help others?

EMMANUEL: Perhaps your goal should be to grow

spiritually, and perhaps you should help yourself. If everyone focused on their own growth, there would be no lost souls.

Journeying inward is your goal, and though you feel such an intense desire to share with others, you need to continue with yourself. Sparks of remembrance come by example, not necessarily by teaching. If you will look back on your own journey, you will recall that it was one individual or one experience that prompted your search. Be a loving being and others will sense your energy and do the same. True growth comes from basking in solitude with oneself.

QUESTIONER: Thank you.

EMMANUEL: You're welcome.

QUESTION: I really enjoy painting, and I've been told I should write. But honestly, I am happy with what I'm doing. I like to be! Sometimes, I wonder, though, if there is something that I should be doing, but generally I am happy where I am at. Should I channel or something?

EMMANUEL: Perhaps you are more aware than you realize. Being is a joyous state. Whatever you choose to do, you will do it well. If you don't want to channel, don't. Spiritual growth comes in many forms. It is all personal and individual. Do not be tricked by the illusion that you must be **doing** something. Being is a state of true oneness, and if you are being, than you are doing quite well.

QUESTION: Emmanuel, I would like to ask a question about my daughter. She seems so unhappy and contrary, and I know somehow that I am creating that. I'd like to know how I can help her and what it is I am doing to create this.

EMMANUEL: She is creating her reality, and you must not blame yourself. You are a very good mother and you have given your children much love. They will always feel that. Your child is a very energetic being (laughing), and I can sense that energy now.

QUESTIONER: She certainly is energetic.

EMMANUEL: Her unruliness is a releasing of that energy. She also has frustrations from previous lives that she will explore when she is older. She is doing what we term "questioning love."

Though you may give her every bit of love you have, she will still doubt its reality. Thus, she challenges you to prove it. You must accept that this is her reality, and this is the way she has chosen to be. Acceptance brings great peace.

She is a very special being, as she will always question and never be told what to think. She needs a lot of love, and you need a little space. Tell her, "I love you very much, but this is something I need and you must respect that." If she is made aware of your needs, she will not feel that you are taking away from hers. Perhaps, in some instances you should try to be more of a friend than a mother. Accept that she will always challenge you. Let go of the illusion that the two of you are creating and grow from it.

QUESTIONER: Thank you very much.

EMMANUEL: You're welcome.

QUESTION: If there was one thing you wanted to say to all of us, what would it be?

EMMANUEL: Love yourself, and give yourself what you need. Don't tell yourself that you don't deserve, or that you are not worthy. You may think, "It's not for me to make that decision or to do this or that." But it is for you. Everything is for you. We desire to help you. YOU ALONE! You are very special and important to us, and we love you very much.

Don't get bogged down in, "What should I accomplish, or what should I do?" You should accomplish happiness, and true happiness comes from a state of being. I cannot tell you how joyful that experience is, as you will not truly experience it until you join me where I am. But, if you allow yourselves, you can visit. (Laughing)

Allow yourselves to experience channeling, astral travel, memory of your past lives, and one-on-one communication with your guides. Our doors are always open!

Remember, what you are here to do is to have fun, to love, to laugh. If you do that, you have done well!

QUESTIONER: Thank you, Emmanuel.

EMMANUEL: You're welcome.

QUESTION: There are so many things I want to do, and I don't feel that until I do those things, I can be happy.

EMMANUEL: May I rephrase your comment? Until you are happy, you will not accomplish the things you wish. (Group laughing)

QUESTIONER: I don't quite see it that way.

EMMANUEL: It is fine to have desires and want to do things, but do not allow those "things" to interfere with what you are doing, and the happiness that you perceive from the now. If that is the way you perceive your reality, then when you do accomplish those things that you so want to do, you will be in the same predicament. You will not experience happiness and joy, because you will always be waiting for some moment in the future. Perhaps, you should try to see every perception along your pathway of life, so that when you do these things, you can be happy then, too.

QUESTIONER: Thank you.

EMMANUEL: You're very welcome.

QUESTION: What is the role I should play with my daughter and her upcoming engagement? I feel that she wants me to interfere somehow and rescue her. How should I handle this situation?

EMMANUEL: As your daughter is creating this for specific growth, it would not be wise for you to interfere. Allow her to deal with her reality and learn from it. It is difficult as a parent to distance yourself from your children, but you must let go and trust the divine plan. She created it for very specific reasons. The most loving thing you can for her is allow her her own reality, whatever that may be.

QUESTION: Did I or anyone here know you when you were on the physical plane?

EMMANUEL: No (laughing), it was long ago.

QUESTIONER: Why are you laughing?

EMMANUEL: I don't want to admit my age.

QUESTIONER: Funny, you don't have wrinkles.

QUESTION: With the recent earthquake in Armenia and the tragic devastation and so many lives lost, can you tell us what causes these tragedies, and what we as a people can do to prevent them? What message does it hold?

EMMANUEL: Respect the thoughts you create and respect the earth. All your thoughts are manifesting in other dimensions, and the consensus reality of mankind creates disasters. The message is to listen, as God is speaking.

Accept that death is an illusion. They have left their physical bodies, but they are still alive and well. Sometimes souls get together and create a tragedy because they are all ready to move on. Having completed their present illusion, they move onto another reality. (Group talks about the sadness of it all)

EMMANUEL: If you could but hear their souls, you would hear great joy. They are experiencing great delight and excitement in what they have found on the other side. The tragedy lies in the physical realm, not in the spiritual. For those in the spiritual realm, there is no tragedy.

QUESTIONER: Thank you.

EMMANUEL: You're welcome. I must go now as the connection is waning due to natural circumstances. (Laughing) I bid you all a good-bye.

(Group says good-bye)

That night Emmanuel channeled through a message for all who might hear him. This is that message.

"My name is Emmanuel. I would like to tell you all of my purpose in channeling through the vessel known as Marilynn. Spiritual entities who channel through the physical realm have varied and different purposes. My purpose in this vessel is to teach of the present, the now, of being-ness, of oneness. My message is simple, and yet quite vast. It is not my purpose to tell you of your past incarnations unless there is present significance. My mind does not encompass names, dates, times and places, as they are all an illusion. I am an emotion-based entity, and I deal with emotions and feelings. That is my purpose. I do not read your mind. I feel your feelings, and I sense your emotions, as that is what is real and truth in my perception. It is simple, it is truth. If you question my existence, then perhaps you should question your own!

"There are different purposes for every channeled entity. Some tell you of the past, some tell you of the future, and I tell you of the now, the present. This is my gift. My purpose is to lead you to yourself, to lead you to the part of you that holds all the answers of your own past, present, and future. My purpose is to lead you to the teacher inside of you, and the spiritual teacher who waits patiently to fill you with all that is, your own spiritual guide. It is your own spiritual guide who holds your file, and it contains everything you ever wanted to know about the being that is you.

"Your purpose is to perceive my message in whatever way is truth for you. If I must prove to you my existence, then my existence is meaningless. So there it is. My purpose is to share my truth, my own ways of perceiving, my oneness, my being-ness and my love with all of you. Your purpose is to open your hearts and allow me to share it with you, and ultimately, discover your own truth and way of perceiving the universe.

All beings are so vastly different, but yet so vastly alike. Beneath the layers of personality, and difference, lies a core of unconditional love, the light in every being. This is what I perceive, this is what I share with you. Embrace it, if you so choose."

CHAPTER TWELVE

CHEYENNE

ASTRAL ORCHESTRATIONS

I began channeling for a group and found myself becoming fearful. Afraid of being exposed or disliked, it was slowing me down.

Flying about the earth out-of-body, my guides left me in an ugly ghetto. The streets were full of litter, a few condemned homes were scattered along the street, and a bare parking lot had become the hangout for a local gang.

Feeling vulnerable, my fear was intense. Some of the gang members started walking towards me, and I began to tremble.

Suddenly, I realized that there was nothing to fear, as they could not see me and I could fly away.

Jutting up towards the sky, I exited the ghetto and headed for the astral plane.

Barrelling down a small walkway, I looked around at the hundreds of entities enjoying themselves. I had entered an astral-plane park, which contained park benches, trees and little meeting areas. Feeling safe, I walked along enjoying the scenery when a female entity approached me.

"You channel Emmanuel! Would you channel him for me and my friends?"

Dragging me to a picnic table underneath a shade tree, she introduced me to her three friends who immediately responded with excitement. "Wow, I am so honored to be in your presence. You must be a great being to channel Emmanuel!" Responding meekly, I tried to tell them I was no different than they, but was interrupted.

"Will you teach us to be enlightened like you?"

Feeling uncomfortable, I told them that they had misunderstood Emmanuel's message. We are all one, and the answers lie within yourself.

The female entity asked some questions about Emmanuel's

message. "Don't you think that unconditional love is impossible to attain? And if we are always experiencing the now, then what about the future?"

Getting angry at these beings who were violating my sacred relationship with Emmanuel, I started to speak, but stopped... The female entity began to smile, her aura of purple and green becoming distinct. She changed her manifestation to that of Emmanuel. "It's you!" I shouted at him, as I laughed at my own delusion. Emmanuel responded, "You fear exposing yourself and being scrutinized. You fear being called a teacher. It scares you to think that others may try to give their power away to you and expect you to know their answers. But, most of all, you fear the expectation of proof. The answer is simple. Be. If you do not take another's power, they cannot give it, and if they desire proof, they do not desire the truth." Pointing in another direction, he told me to follow the path. He stood and disappeared.

Walking along, I noticed a holographic image of my husband up ahead. The image was being rude to an entity for whom I had great respect. Running up to the entity, I apologized for my husband's behavior. "He didn't mean it, he often overreacts." But the entity wanted nothing more to do with the wife of someone so rude. I remembered this was a fear of mine. My husband had used this type of manipulation to interfere with my friendships and I was afraid he might do it to my new friends in the metaphysical community.

Continuing down the path, my little girl joined me. We flew together for a short while, and then I focused my attention to what lay ahead. Exiting the park, I planned to re-enter my body. Looking to my side, my child was no longer there and I panicked. I returned to the park and found her being tended to by other entities. Quickly picking her up, I took her back to the earth-plane. My fear was of not meeting my child's needs, and it was important that I evaluate whatever work I chose, so that my baby doll would have plenty of love.

Contemplating this visit, I evaluated my fears and vowed to overcome them. Andy acknowledged his manipulative behavior and joined with me in our goal to remove it.

THE CREATIVE ZONE

Flying through the dimensions, I happened upon the plane

of inspiration and creativity. A totally white dimension, beings performed their musical visions of light on podiums scattered all about the space. Astral instruments, some resembling those we have on earth and others very different, produced a beautiful sound unattainable in the physical realm. The melodies meshed together to form celestial sounds of unimaginable excitement!

Walking along the white pathways, I noticed a sax player engulfed in his music. Entranced by his song, I stopped to listen. I didn't immediately recognize this entity, but he was a stockpile friend.

Finishing up, he came to talk to me and we embraced in the happiness at seeing each other again. The stockpile visit was for him, however, as I was the one who had "hurt" him. He had been engaged to my best friend for years, who suddenly left him for another man and got married. Torn between loyalties, I lost touch with him.

In our embrace, he knew that I had meant him no harm. Feeling the love I had for him, he had no need to ask questions. I had cherished our friendship, and he could not deny that feeling. Smiling, he returned to his sax playing, the love evident.

Traversing the mystical walkway, I listened to the soulful sounds of the celestial beings I passed.

Returning to my body, I awoke.

Parting with my body a few days later, I returned to the creative zone accompanied by a female entity who I perceived as a guide. We were going to perform in a trio together. Coming upon an empty podium where we were to play, a beautiful Indian being walked up, the third in our trio. My guide played the flute, and I was to play the bassoon, but I couldn't. Mesmerized, I stared at the Indian with beautiful black hair and olive skin. A bit stocky, he was not very tall. The two began to play, and a third entity came in to take my place on the bassoon. As they played, understanding came. This beautiful Indian was a middle-man between me and my Indian master.

Celestial music filling my being, the male and female entities smiled and disappeared, leaving me with the Indian. Putting his arm around me, he led me down the corridors of light, which were tunnel-like hallways that glowed with white-light. As I was so happy to be with this entity, I began to cry tears of joy. His energy filled me with peace.

A thought-form Indian woman appeared with a small baby, his wife and child. They disappeared quickly, and I realized that he was showing me our connection to each other.

Entering a small private room, we both lay down together on what appeared to be nothing. "You wanted to experience what it means to be. I will show you what being-ness is, lay your head on my shoulder and be." Doing as he said, I felt the most intense love, peace and joy I had ever experienced! My being pulsated with love and light, and I could not be more content. As we enjoyed **being** together, other entities would pop by, smiling and leaving when they realized we were being. There was such great respect given to us in our state of being, whereas in the physical plane you are expected to always be doing something. Sharing and receiving energy, we lay there for hours and I had no desire to do anything else.

When we finished, we both headed down another corridor of light. "It is important for you to receive these energies so that you will be able to meet with the Indian master," he said. Entering a large, white, crowded room, he took me over to a bookshelf. Opening a book about Indians, he said, My name is CHEYENNE, as I was a Cheyenne Indian. I will call you Ute. With a hug, he bid me to return to my body.

CLYDESDALES

Attending an astral support group on a beach, two gals and a guy were discussing their latest crisis. Sitting quietly, I did not participate.

One of the women began to speak of her late boyfriend who had been murdered a few weeks earlier. "I don't know what to do, I want to avenge his death, but I just don't know what's right." The other woman began to respond, but suddenly looked up at me and said, "Well, what do you think she should do?"

Looking at the woman with as much compassion and understanding as I could muster, I responded, "It would be difficult to tell you anything at this time, as it happened so recently. However, the most loving thing you can do is to let him go. This is his past-life, and he needs for you to allow him space to move on. Everything that happened was planned, and you need to put it all in the hands of God."

Disintegrating, I passed through the time tunnel and into another lifetime.

Working in a Russian shop, I was a young boy in my teens. I worked with an older man who wore an apron and leaned forward with a hunch. Running a manual machine making horse reins, I was his apprentice. The shop supplied all the needs for horses and sleighs. As the snow fell hard in the high country, the horse and sleigh were our main transportation.

Moments later, I was dropped into a beautiful sleigh which was pulled by two light brown Clydesdale horses. The snow was falling and the forest floor was a blanket of white. Enjoying the ride, we followed the path through the woods.

Pulled from the scene, I flew through the tunnel and entered my body.

CHANNELING NOTE

Three more group sessions and one private session occurred before I moved on to my Indian master.

Saying many of the same things, I have not included the transcripts, but would like to share a few notes.

Some friends of ours, Theresa and Steve, compose beautiful music, and we have been fans of theirs for a long time. Emmanuel shared with them that they are channeling music from the inspirational and creative realms. We had joined forces in helping this couple to pursue their musical dream of recording New Age music. Emmanuel wanted this to happen, as their music is inspired and part of the plan to bring in the New Age. Later, I would begin work in the spiritual realm to bring this about.

In response to the question, "When will I meet my soul-mate, and why have I not met her yet?," Emmanuel responded with important words. "You do not love yourself, and until you love yourself, you will never truly love another. If you were to meet your soul-mate today, would you be able to love her as you would like to be loved? I think not. Learn to love others, by learning to love yourself. When you do this, your soul-mate will come into your life.

SPIRITUAL SONAR

Undergoing another vibrational raising, I completely surrendered and let it happen. When it was over, I left my body, and went to visit my brother.

My brother is a great guy, but has no belief in God. Living in Cincinnati, he had a one-bedroom apartment. When I arrived, no one was there, and I didn't even know where I was. Waiting, I looked around wondering why I was sent here.

Walking into the apartment, my brother had two spiritual entities with him. One was a guide, and the other was his deceased best friend. This guy had been a real mischievous person while living, and it seemed that nothing had changed, as he motioned me to join in on the fun!

Flying about the room raising the energy, his friend was pinching him, but my brother was determined not to acknowledge either of us. Even his subconscious mind did not respond. Finishing up, we left the apartment and went our separate ways.

THE CIRCLE OF LIFE

Emmanuel taught me this lesson in the empty space dimension via thought-form, and I would like to share it with you.

Several people lined up in a circle and put their arms on each other's shoulders. Music began and they all began to dance around their circle of life. Asking them to stop, Emmanuel told them, "Look around you and tell me, who were the followers and who were the leaders?" The people all looked, and could not decide. Each person in the circle was doing both. "Let this be a lesson to you. Know that you will always have things of the spirit to share with others, but that you should constantly follow the beckoning of your inner soul, as there will always be more to learn."

KIDNAPPING!

Cruising through the time tunnel, I entered into the body of a pregnant oriental woman. It appeared to be the early twentieth century.

A man was with me, white, tall, and muscular with brown hair, and we were lovers. Giving birth to twins, I planned to raise them alone. A few days after their birth, one of the twins was kidnapped by his father who sold him for money.

Dropped into a point two years later, I tracked down my former boyfriend at a university, and with a little effort, found that he had given the child to a professor and his wife. Sitting in the speakers' hall listening to the professor give a speech, I turned to leave and saw my former boyfriend. Confronting him and the professor, he admitted his guilt, and the professor returned the child to me.

Pulled out of the body, I was watching from above. The former lover appeared next to me asking forgiveness. Realizing that this was a past-life stockpile situation, I told him that I had forgiven him long ago. Feeling a strong love from him, he said, "I never forgot you and I always regretted what I did. You taught me how to love, and I will be forever grateful for that." Responding with a hug, I told him I understood and had loved him very much, too. Going through the tunnel, there was more to do.

Waiting in a realm with a very high vibrational level, I noticed a pale blue color seemed to permeate the entire dimension. Suddenly, a beautiful distant voice could be heard. It was my Indian master! Unable to understand his voice, I felt crushed by the power of his high vibration. Not yet ready to meet him, I returned to my physical body.

BLENDING INTO ONE

After leaving my body, I met Emmanuel. My friend Theresa, and my husband, were both there, subconscious astral. The dimension beamed with a yellowish-white light and the feelings of love were total.

Emmanuel taught us about oneness by having us experience it. As we all were beings of light, we were transparent yellow-white lights with a revolving core. Melding into my being, Emmanuel and I blended into one entity. Doing the same with my husband and Theresa, Emmanuel then blended all of us together, the four now one.

When two souls are blended, they appear to be one soul. A flash of light can be seen when the two become one. It is an extremely beautiful and loving experience and I felt very blessed to have been a part of it.

After the other two had left, Emmanuel spoke to me, "They

will not remember this when they awake, and I want you to tell them about it. Theresa is not aware of it, yet, but I wish to teach her. Tell her this." Nodding in agreement, I turned to leave.

MOBSTER STOCKPILE

After speaking with Red Jacket about getting together and doing something fun, he took me out of my body and to a snow covered mountain. Flying up the hill, sometimes permeating the snow, and other times flying so high into the heavens that we could see the whole of the earth, we enjoyed ourselves immensely. The snow was very deep and we traveled through caverns, up rocks, and by trees. When we reached the top, we flew down like sleigh riders with no need for a sleigh! After we were through partying, Red Jacket took me to the empty space dimension, and left me all alone.

Surrounded by spirits from my mob lifetime, I began to feel frightened. They did nothing, and their inaction made me nervous. Over a time, I calmed down, realizing that there was no immediate danger.

One of the entities spoke, "We want you to know that we are very sorry that we killed you and your husband. As you know, our actions came as a result of our illusion, and we have all grown and evolved since that time. We do love you very much, and we hope that you can forgive us and let this go." Understanding that they were no threat to anyone any more, I thanked them for taking the time to work this out with me. Forgiving them, I returned to the physical.

ROMAN LIFE WITH RED JACKET

An interesting karmic twist occurred when I traveled through the time tunnel into a Roman life with Red Jacket. In this lifetime, I was the prisoner!

Entering into the body of a dark-haired woman, I saw a gorgeous man with blonde hair at my side. It was the being Red Jacket. He was a guard at a slave camp for women, and he was very tall and muscular. Angry and resisting, I had just been captured and brought to this place. The place was built very sparsely as they only provided minimum needs for the prisoners. This was part of an illegal slave operation, and the women were sold to wealthy men. To make it even more profitable, they had the women working in the fields until they were sold, and they could sell their crops to the far-away towns. This would be their downfall, as people would become suspicious of the source of their crops and take action.

The gorgeous guard had a reputation for fooling around with a lot of the female inmates, and one night he came to visit me in my hut-like cell. Telling him I wasn't interested, we ended up talking all night long and becoming very close friends.

It didn't take long for us to fall in love, and as a result, my life became a lot easier. Surprised that he had fallen for a woman this way, he became very protective of me and made sure that I didn't get sold. One of his jobs was to provide water from the well, and in order to get me out of field work, he had me help him.

Out of nowhere, the camp was attacked by soldiers, as someone had figured out that these guys were kidnapping women and selling them as slaves. Women were running everywhere trying to escape during the uproar, and after waiting a short time for my man to come, I decided I must go, too. Frantically running out of the camp, I heard his voice calling me. Turning, he motioned me to return, but several other guards were running after us. This was my only chance, and I took it. He stayed to defend his world, and I took off to find what was left of mine.

Popping out of the body, I saw him sitting in my hut. An incredible sadness showing on his face, one lone teardrop slowly fell on his cheek.

Returning to my body, I pondered this little karmic twist.

CHAPTER THIRTEEN
KUTAHEY!

ASTRAL CONVENTION

Cruising out of my body, I went to a large space on the astral plane for two conventions of subconscious astrals.

In the first convention, about one hundred people from my high school class showed up, and I began speaking of truth. Telling them that they could venture inward and do wonderful things, they responded with some religious tenets of the Catholic church. When told that they could astral project, they began to immediately laugh. "What are you, some kind of nut? That astral projection stuff is a bunch of garbage!" Smiling at them, I replied, "Is that so...hmm". Well, would it make it any clearer if I told you that you are all out of your bodies right now?" In a wild state of panic, several entities noticed their transparent nature. "Oh, my God. How will I get back to my body!" Calming them, I told them to will themselves home, and they would be fine.

The next group was a gay convention and they were much more open to reality. As I stood on the podium and talked of truth, they cheered with the enthusiasm of a crowd at a Super Bowl game. After a while of discussing astral projection and unconditional love, I left the scene for a well-deserved rest.

Red Jacket picked me up and took me to the northern polar ice cap. As you feel no temperature in your astral body, it was not cold. Sliding on the ice and into the water, we had a great time for several hours. After jumping in some snowdrifts, Red Jacket led me home to my body.

A VISIT TO THE PLANET ASHTAR

On Christmas Eve, Andy (subconscious astral) and I prepared for a special trip. The neighbor baby came over astrally to play with Melissa, and we left the scene.

Out of our bodies, we went to the ocean and enjoyed the beautiful sounds of the waves hitting shore. Having asked Emmanuel to help me to accept those who choose to ignore reality, he told us a story.

"Notice how vast the ocean is and how many drops of water exist out there. Every few moments, some of those drops come into shore on a wave. A small amount in comparison to the size of the vast sea, but they come in to see if there truly is such a thing as a shore.

"They have heard stories about a shore, but all they have known is the vast expanse of the sea. Some of those drops come in, look, and say, 'No, I am only dreaming,' and rush back to sea. But a few of those drops see the shore, grab onto a piece of sand, and say, 'It is real! There really is a shore!' In their excitement, they beckon to the ocean, 'I have found truth, the shore exists, it is real!' But the drops of water far out to sea think it is only an impossible dream. Other drops continually come and go, some finding the shore, others frightened by what they see. The drops who so want to share the truth of the shore continue to beckon, and in frustration, get angry at the drops further out. 'How can you be so blind? The shore is right in front of your eyes!'

"A voice inside of them tells them, 'Only a small amount of water can hold onto the sand. The beaches are small in comparison to the wide expanse of the sea. You have made it to shore, now move on, my friend, and make room for another drop to fill your space. Help them by letting them find the shore themselves. But do not stop beckoning, as the stories of the great shore are what lead them to question its existence.'

"So the drop evaporated into the sky and made room for another drop to grab onto the shore. From above, he saw a tiny drop fill his former space and find truth. Then the drop shed his physical shell, and in his place a tiny soul came. It rained, and the new soul began his journey to find the shore.

"Remember, my friend, continue to beckon, but move on and allow others the space to find their own truth. It is all a great flowing plan, and each will find truth in his own time. We love you in your imperfection, love those who are confused, as we love you." Leaving Andy at the peaceful ocean, I flew up into the sky and journeyed towards the stars.

Flying through the blackness of space, the stars rushed by as I ventured to a faraway planet. Reaching my destination, an astral spaceship orbiting the planet Ashtar, I looked around. My friend Vickie channels an entity from Astar, and I felt this may have something to do with her. In the small, silver craft, a being manifesting as a blonde, human female, was communicating with someone on a radio device. A disagreement ensued, and she cut off communications turning to speak with me.

"I have a message for Vickie. She may be physically contacted by another life-form, and I don't want her to respond. This being comes from a scientifically evolved society, rather than a spiritually evolved society. They view human beings the same way you people view animals. Though they mean her no harm, they will not help her in any way. I will send you to see this entity, so that you may describe him to her."

Beamed onto another spaceship, I saw an entity with two large black eyes, a big cranium with no hair, wearing a black robe. He looked like the drawing on the cover of the book *Communion*, but he was completely white and of average human height. The spaceship was obviously physical, rather than the astral one I had just left. Leaving the scene I returned through the stars to meet my husband on the beach. Taking his hand, we returned to our physical bodies.

After telling Vickie of the experience, she told me that the entities she channels do transmit directly from an astral spaceship orbiting the planet. Apparently, she had been told by a psychic that she might be contacted by another intelligence. This was confirming for her, and she was ready to take steps to avoid that reality.

EMMANUEL'S ASCENT

While walking into the bathroom one night, a beautiful bright ball of light came down in the colors of white and purple. Rotating rapidly, it expanded in light and manifested as a being of light. It was Emmanuel, and he spoke, "I want you to channel for some small groups, and I want Andy to be there. It is the only way we can reach him now, and I would like it to begin right away. Nodding in acknowledgement, I turned to go to bed. Andy blurted out, "He's here! Emmanuel's here, I feel him!" Smiling, I told him of our rendezvous.

I went to sleep and left my body. Passing through the time tunnel, I made a quick visit into another Indian lifetime.

Riding a horse frantically through a small western town, I was escaping from the white man. An Indian woman, my hair was braided and I wore a buffalo skin dress.

Up ahead, I saw three Crow Indian men and rode towards them, hoping they would help me in my escape. They turned and galloped away, and I followed. Riding through the prairie grass, they entered into a plot of woods. "Why didn't they wait for me," I wondered, but I continued to follow. Losing them in the woods, I turned around and got off my horse. Bending over, one of the Indians placed an axe in my back. Pain searing through me, I tried to leave my body, but I hadn't died, yet. It didn't take long, though, as only moments later I escaped the painful condition.

Meeting me on the astral plane, the Indian responsible asked me to forgive him. He had been misled by the whites, and went against his own people. Recognizing this entity as the same entity who showed me the map of my spiritual journey, I knew his intentions were good. "Of course I forgive you, and I thank you for the help you are giving me now." With that he hugged me, leaving that reality behind. Soaring through the tunnel, I went home.

TRANSITIONS

Out of my body, I went to an eerie old mansion where a man named Sam lived. Sam was a musician, and he sold insurance as a cover for his illegal activities. The two great loves in his life were his Great Dane Dog and his Whalefish. Once in a while, he dabbled in astral travel, but never left the earth-plane.

Watching Sam, I realized that I was one of his spirit guides, and he was one of the souls I worked with in-between lives.

Traveling a lot, Sam spent little time in his home. His two best friends, a young couple, took care of the place while he was away. Simple people, they did it because of their friendship for Sam. They didn't care for the mansion and enjoyed a less complicated life.

Sam had left the two in charge of the house for a couple of weeks, and he was running late in his return. The woman had a dream that Sam died, and she called some people to confirm.

Dying in his sleep, his will left everything he owned to the couple. Surprised, they didn't really want it.

Deluged with lawyers and agents, everyone wanted to disavow Sam's will and get in on the estate. Some were saying that Sam was crazy because of his interest in astral travel. Others complained of the care that the couple had given the home.

In a dream, the woman received a phone call from the spirit world. Sam wanted them to have the estate because he knew they would do something good with it. Having a new perspective, Sam wanted the home to be used for something worthwhile. The same night, everyone involved gathered, subconscious astral, in the huge auditorium of the house. Planning on being born into his new lifetime as a nun within a few hours, Sam wanted this to be resolved. I assured him that everything would be okay, and we joined the group.

Manifesting as a medium-size, white man in my twenties, I walked in and spoke to the group about astral projection. Their reaction was one of disbelief, as they were not aware that I was a spirit. Appearing to the group, Sam flew about the room to gauge their reactions. Some of the people blocked, but most were seeing this through their own window of perception. Just then, I soared towards the sky flying about the room. Spreading love energy to everyone, I began to speak. "Your physical world is an illusion. All there is, is unconditional love. You are not judged, and there is no hell. Fear is what allows you to deny this. Sam wants these two people to have this property, as they will do with it something valuable. To deny this is to deny your own illusory laws. All there is, is love!" After landing from my love flight, a short, bent-over, old man came to me in tears and embraced my being. Surprised, but undaunted by my lack of physical form, the tears flowed in a glowing confirmation of the love of God. Spending a moment to be with this man, we shared energies and I left the earth-plane.

The estate was settled the next day and the couple donated the huge mansion to the Catholic church to become an orphanage. Changing his mind, Sam decided to become a priest and was born a boy.

Four years later Sam's parents died in an accident, and he was taken to the Catholic orphanage. Looking around the huge home, Sam came upon a maintenance man. "What was this building used for before it became an orphanage?" he asked. "A very rich man owned this house, and he lived here all alone," he replied.

"But why would anyone want to live in a house this big all by themselves?" Sam asked. The maintenance man shrugged his shoulders to say he did not know, and Sam continued. "Well, I'm glad that old man realized that this place could be a good home for people like us. It's fun having all my friends live here with me sharing everything." My job finished, I flew off and returned to my present existence.

GUARDIAN SPIRITS

Flying out of my body, I underwent a fear journey. Passing through ghettos and running into thought-forms, I felt very unsafe for the moment.

All alone in an astral amphitheater, I manifested a dark robe covering my entire being. Sitting with my head bowed down, contemplating, a noticeable presence could be felt coming from behind. I meekly turned to see who it was. Shimmering in his Roman sachet, a beautiful entity stood. Manifesting long, sandy hair, beautiful biceps, and sandals on his feet, a light of bright yellow shone all around him. The warmth of his energy made me feel like melting into this being. Smiling, he spoke, "I am your guardian spirit. Why do you fear?" Looking in awe at this beautiful being, I could not answer. "No harm will ever come to you, as I will protect you always." Reaching out to him, our hands met in a shimmering bolt of light. In the blink of an eye, we were at an ocean and we rode the waves for a little while. When it was time to return, he said, "I am always there for you. If you allow yourself to feel my presence, you will know that you are safe." A love thought-form was exchanged and I returned to my body.

KUTAHEY!

Emmanuel spoke to me before leaving my body. "I now set you free, my little bird with golden wings, may your wings span the entire universe! I give this being of light to the Indian master, Kutahey!" When he finished, I knew that my days with Emmanuel were finished. I had graduated.

Leaving my body, I entered into an interesting thought-

form. Groups of people from my past and present were all
working together, and they were angry with me as I was not
working with them. In my frustration I responded, "Don't you
see? Who I was a year ago is not who I am today!" They
couldn't understand, and they asked me to leave. "I like you
the way you are, why is it so difficult to like me the way I am?
Am I really so different?" I said, almost in tears. I knew I had
to leave and exited through a side door.

One of my stockpile friends was sitting alone in a thought-
form room. Hurt and upset that his father was in trouble, he
wanted to know how to help him. To further his frustration,
he was not able to see the being who had the answer. Asking
him why, he looked at me in excitement, "But, you can! The
being is behind that door, [he pointed behind him] would you
talk with him?" Smiling, I replied, "Of course I will go, maybe
he can help you." Permeating the door, I floated into the room.

Inside a beautiful entity sat behind a small table. Manifesting as a small, oriental, bald man wearing a robe, he immediately looked my way and smiled. Respectfully, I spoke. "My
friend is having a very serious problem with his father, and
he feels that you know what he should do." Pausing to look
at me a moment, the entity asked, "Why do you feel so
strongly about finding an answer for this entity, what does he
mean to you?" "Well," I responded, "I love him very much,
and I think I understand his despair, as my own father was
very much like his. I could never help him, and had to leave
him to his own reality." The entity laughed, "My child, you
are wiser than you realize. Perhaps you could have given him
an answer yourself. Did you realize that when you feel such
love for another being, you then feel it for yourself? In that
state of loving completely, all answers come to you. All the
answers are simple." The being asked me if I understood the
thought-form I put myself through. "No, I did not. It was very
frustrating for me." The being replied, "My child, you experience frustration in your physical world because people
don't see who you are. They don't see who you are, because
they don't see who they are. They cannot forgive others,
because they do not forgive themselves. Their disappointment is real, but it is not at you, but themselves. Having not
accepted that all the answers lie within, they find—none.
Believing unconditional love to be too simple, they do not

become a part of the divine energy of love that flows through every being. They still try to do rather than **flow.**

"My dear friend, you have chosen to flow with the divine plan of oneness and love. We do things *through* you, rather than *by* you. Few will see that in your world, so you must see it yourself. Recognize this, and your frustration will turn into understanding and love."

Thanking this great being, I turned to leave, but he stopped me. "Wait, my friend, I desire to speak with you more. Will you return?" "Of course," I responded, "but why do you want to talk to me? After all, I am not anywhere near your level of evolution!" The beautiful being laughed, "I want to teach you, I am Kutahey!" Thrilled and excited, I asked, "But you do not look the same as before. You appeared as an American Indian, and now you look like a man from India. Which one are you?" Patiently, he replied, "What I am, is who you are. Cannot I be both, and more! Do not limit your perception of me. Go through the door that you have entered, and confront your fearful thought-form. If you can enter into understanding and love, it will disappear and be replaced by whatever beauty you desire. We will meet again!"

Floating through the door, the friend who needed help was no longer there. Appearing to me for an instant, he said,"I have found the answer inside myself. Thank you." A thought-form of love was exchanged and I wished him well.

The thought-form people were still there, angry as ever and preparing to confront me. Looking their way, I replied, "Your anger is not at me, but yourselves. Understand who you are, and you will understand who I am." Lying on the ground, I turned off my sight. When I willed it to return, they were no longer there, replaced by a beautiful snow-capped mountain. I lay in the grass looking up at the blue sky. Knowing who I was, I freed myself from my own delusion. After enjoying the scenery, I went back to my body.

CHAPTER FOURTEEN

SPEAKING WITH JESUS

THE PREACHER

Cruising out of my body, I was led to watch a fundamentalist preacher. Acting as his spirit guide, I scanned over parts of his life to prepare myself for his impending death.

A very hateful man, he used fear to influence people to join his congregation. A longstanding feud existed between him and another minister who believed in a loving God. The two churches helped each other out by sharing some of their supplies, but the preacher violated this relationship many times. Unable to convert the other minister to his way, he would withhold church music and displays. An older, balding and small man, he died of cardiac arrest in his pulpit preaching hell-fire and damnation.

As his spirit rose to meet me, I looked at him very lovingly. "Fearing God, you never found him. Fearing truth, you never understood. In your ego, you took power from others, and in your blindness, you saw only evil." Pausing a moment, the entity looked at me in confusion. I continued, "When you look at me, what do you see?" Thinking a moment, he replied, "Love, I feel so much love!" Smiling at the being, I responded, "Now you have truth!" Taking the being to the light, I left him with one last message, "Remember my words when you choose your next lifetime." Beaming, happy, I watched the being enter paradise. Returning to my body, I awoke.

TUNNELS TO INFINITY

Flying out of my body, I was enjoying the night air. Finding myself in an unusual place, I noticed there were two staircases leading up a mountain of rock. Cruising up tho long staircase on the right, it led to a flat rock podium. My mother, sister, and brother were there, all subconscious astral. Behind them in the rock wall, were two tunnels. Soaring through the air, I showed them how much fun it is to fly. Doing flips and other tricks, my family was excited.

Suddenly, the tunnel on the right beckoned me to enter. Following my instinct, I flew inside. This was the tunnel to infinity where all of our probable futures lie. After what seemed like miles, I came across a probable future where my mother was dying in a house-fire. One of my siblings was there, too. Understanding, I turned back. All of a sudden, dead bodies began to spring up from the floor of the tunnel. Immediately realizing it as a fear, they turned into mannequins. Laughing at my own distortion of reality, I continued.

Upon return to the podium, I hovered above them and described their probable future. Using physical words, as they could not tune into my telepathic communication, I explained what had to be done. "The two tunnels represent the twin-ness of man. The right tunnel contains our negative futures, and the left, our positive futures. In order to change this negative probability, you must enter the tunnel on the left and re-create it through thought-forms."

Awkwardly, they manipulated their astral bodies into the tunnel and I left the scene. Passing through the time tunnel, I came upon a parallel lifetime.

Entering into the body of an Air Force enlisted woman, I was watching a superior officer setting a bomb. A friend of mine was with me, and she witnessed the whole event. As a series of sabotaging incidents had plagued the base, we decided to go to a higher authority with the information. Immediately detained, we were locked up and mistreated. Charged with insubordination for ratting on a superior officer, my anger brewed.

A handsome high ranking officer came into tho building where we were held, and I immediately went on a rampage about the ridiculous treatment we were getting. The officer was tall with straight, graying, slicked, black hair and stunning features. Responding quickly, he ordered all the charges to be dropped, and he had mo appointed to the investigation team, which he led.

The officer and I quickly fell in love, but I found out that he was married. His wife was in a coma, and had boon for several years. Lying in a hospital bed, she was all but dead, and we continued our romance. Catching the guy who sabotaged the base, we were given commendations. While sharing a loving hug, I was pulled from tho body.

Flying into yet another body, I realized I was living out a probable future for my present life.

Widowed with my child and living in Texas, I was unhappy being a working mom. Worrying incessantly about her care, I was a miserable moss. Looking up, I asked my guides to take mo back to the two tunnels of infinity so that I could change this probable future. Their voices spoke in my head, "You do not need to visit the tunnels of infinity, as you are an enlightened being and can change this reality consciously." Excited by that truth, I popped out of the probable future and destroyed it with thought-forms. Returning to my body, I awoke.

As all of us who inhabit physical bodies have dark corners, it is important to confront them consciously and destroy their illusory reality, thus freeing yourself to light.

THE RECORD PRODUCER

Out of my body, I went to join an astral support group. The people in the group were interested in hearing Emmanuel, and I explained that he no longer channeled through me at will. Looking at it as a sideshow, their only interest was to see someone channel. It did not matter what tho entity had to say. A man with wavy medium-length hair, balding on top, manifesting a cigar in his mouth, approached another woman in the group. "I'm a record executive and I can make you a famous channel, why don't you try to channel for us?" While she thought about it, the record man left her alone and came to speak with me.

When he pressured me to channel, I told the man that if Emmanuel wanted to come through, he would let me know. "Channeling is not a game, it is a gift given by the spiritual realm. When you are ready to hear Emmanuel's message, he will be ready to speak with you." Getting a little upset with me, he responded, "How can you take all that love stuff seriously?!" Walking away from the producer, a young priest came up to me. With desire pouring out of his being, he peacefully replied, "May I speak with Emmanuel?" A gush of energy pulsated my being, and I knew the time was right.

Going into trance, I channeled, and when I returned, the

priest was greatly moved. Thanking me, he embraced me and left. Glancing at the record executive, I knew he had been changed. "I would like to record Emmanuel," he said with a new-found respect. Thinking a moment, I responded, "The power of Emmanuel is not only in his words, but his presence. That cannot be felt from a tape, but let me tell you what Emmanuel would like. I have these two friends, Theresa and Steve, who channel celestial music from the inspirational realm. It is Emmanuel's desire that their music be brought out to the world, as it carries a high spiritual vibration. When people listen to their music, they will be moved." Looking at me with a confused look on his face, he turned to think and I left.

Looking for a good time, I cruised through tho sky. Down below, two men were riding some beautiful horses, and I quickly descended towards tho astral beings. One of them motioned me to come down, and rescinded his horse, leaving the scene. The horse was a beautiful brown and we galloped through tho skies trying all sorts of rodeo tricks. In my etheric body, I didn't have to think about getting hurt. When we finished, we both hugged our horses and watched them fly off into the universe. Speaking to the other rider, I found that he had a wife and five kids but one of his children had died. Leaving the scene, I had no idea that we would meet again very soon.

A few days later, I left my body and went directly to this man's home. It was a teenage daughter who had died, and the two parents met me in their living room, subconscious astral. "Your daughter is alive and well, but is now visible to another dimension. She created this reality and was ready to move on. We all return to earth many times to learn different lessons, and the most important lesson of all is unconditional love. She did this for you, too. You can grow from her death, by learning to trust." His wife had heard enough and returned to her body, but my friend stayed. A handsome guy of about 40 years, he had sandy brown hair feathered back on his head and he was very tall. "I don't think I am ready to accept all this, yet," he said, "Is that okay?" Smiling at him, I said, "Of course. You take all the time you need. Remember, though, that as soon as you are able to accept this reality, your daughter will be able to communicate with you. This is some-thing she desires."

Meeting a friend of mine, subconscious astral, in Texas, I tried to talk with her. Immediately upset by my presence, she created thought-form phones, "We can't talk like this! We live too far away from each other. How did you do this?!" Realizing that she was not ready to meet with me, I flew off and went to a desert.

Tumbleweeds blew by, and the cactus flowers bloomed in the beautiful astral desert. Feeling the oneness and being-ness with all that is, I sat with myself and enjoyed the beauty of this place. Suddenly, an old friend that I had not seen in years, rode by on a thought-form dirt bike, waving. Returning

the greeting, I noticed an especially beautiful crimson red flower in bloom on a large cactus. Moments later, I returned to my body.

THE RETURN OF THE LOST SOUL

While traveling out of my body, I ran into Laurie Dann's reality. Laurie was an escaped mental patient who entered an elementary school, shot several students and then took her own life.

In her reality, Laurie was shooting at several thought-form children running back and forth between two school buses. Walking towards her, my presence evoked the same anger with her as it did with the suicide months before. Shooting at me viciously with her thought-form gun, I continued my slow approach as the bullets flew right through me. A look of fear came across her face as she realized she had no control over me as she did with her thought-form children.

Walking right up to her, she turned, putting her arms over her eyes. I put my arm around her and sat with her. Embracing her with my being, I sent love energies to her. Without saying a word, we sat in a state of being-ness and waited until she accepted the love.

Moments later, an attractive male entity appeared with brown hair, a moustache, and very tall. Manifesting in a police uniform, he was one of Laurie's guides and was here to "take her away." The police get-up would be easier for her to accept.

He spoke to me, "Why don't we get together after your next assignment and go mountain climbing?" Nodding in agreement, I was whisked to my next job and he took Laurie to the light.

As I watched a family from above, the parents were plotting to kill their five-year-old son. Traumatized from his past-lives, the child was destructive and dangerous. He had tried to kill his parents, and he enjoyed setting fire to the home. Unable to deal with him, the parents electrocuted him in a bathtub.

As he began to create a thought-form reality, I intervened. He was throwing a fit of anger, feeling unworthy of love. I floated to him and embraced him. "I love you," I said calmly sharing my energy with the soul. Struggling for a few moments, he didn't want to believe it, but knew that it was true. Pointing at his guides, I said, "They love you, too."

Reaching out their hands, they took the little boy home.

The guide from the previous job appeared and took my hand in a flash of light. Beaming to a beautiful rock mountain-top, we sat and rejuvenated our spirits. "You know," he said, "This is a great place to go after a day at work. It re-energizes your being." Comforting my tired being, he added, "Next time I have a lost soul to deal with, I am going to look you up! You are very good at handling them. Do you know why?" My tired face looked up at him and I said no. He continued, "Do you have any idea why you created so much turmoil in the first half of this lifetime?

"Well", I responded, "probably because I'm an idiot." Laughing, he said, "You really don't see it, do you? When you deal with these lost souls, you are able to access memories from this lifetime, and truly understand their pain. Those souls know that what you offer them is real understanding.

Most importantly, your love for them is real, and it is this that breaks their delusion." I looked up, "Do you mean to say that I chose these hardships to prepare myself for my work with the lost souls?" Nodding that this was the case, he gave me a hug. "I know you don't recognize who I am, but you are very special to me. We have known each other for a long time." As we flew down the mountain, we sent each other thought-forms of love, and headed back to our present realities.

AN OFFICE LUNCH

Entering into a thought-form reality, I became part of a

group dream. In some instances, dreams are astral experiences performed through thought-forms.

In a high-rise building, four women were meeting for lunch. Sitting at their table gossiping about the days events, they were surprised when I casually sat with them. Not speaking, they continued but became increasingly bothered by my presence. One of the women looked at me and asked, "What did you do to create such a bright light around you?" Smiling contentedly, I replied, "I am flowing with the divine plan of unconditional love and existing in a state of peace and being."

The women stared at me in silence as I stood and disappeared into the air.

Leaving the scene, another lost soul beckoned. A black man was being killed in the electric chair, and I was summoned to his aid. As he left his body and entered the astral state, I embraced the being and welcomed him to the other side. Angry, he said, "All right, where am I going to be sent now?" Obviously assuming he was going to some sort of hell, I told him there was only love. Breaking our embrace, he paced, "Wait a minute, that's crazy!- I waited patiently for him to absorb this truth. "Okay", I can handle it, tell me more.- I explained everything to him and told him he was greatly loved. As his guides descended in wispy light forms, he reached out his hand to them.

Pausing, he turned to say thanks and followed his guides to the light!

After visiting some sub-conscious astral friends, I went back to my body and awoke.

JESUS CHRIST

Cruising through a pastel blue dimension, I saw a light beaming down through the sky from another plane. Asking some of the entities hanging around what it was, they told me to touch the light and Jesus would speak to me.

As I did it, a sudden, massive energy surge pulsated my being and a powerful voice spoke. "My dear one, you come to me with fear and worry. Let us understand what you fear so as not to hide your light."

In a thought-form, unaware entities came to speak with Jesus. But, because of their doubt, the connection waned, and Jesus did not speak. Hurt that they could not appreciate this beautiful gift, I felt there should be a way that I could help them to see.

Jesus spoke again, "Don't expect to be validated by the earth-plane, just feel strength within yourself and do the tasks you have set out to do. You may be misunderstood even by those you respect as teachers. Some of them are so involved in the monetary aspect of what they do, they no longer see, and they may perceive you as a threat. If only they knew that you represent what they could become You will lead beings to themselves, thus, away from their lucrative businesses.

"I have a task for you that you will become aware of when the time comes. Remember that your growth is of tho utmost importance, as our task will depend on your continuing evolution. Don't stop for anyone, as venturing forth will force others to follow your lead and venture inward themselves. You are greatly loved, and I am very proud of your progress. Let your light shine brightly!"

Taking a short pause, he continued, Marilynn, why do you think we are able to speak with you?" Confused, I responded, "I really don't know. Knowing that I have just as many faults and imperfections as everyone else, it has left me wondering. . . ." He interrupted, "We are able to speak with you because you put your ego aside and ask to be told the truth. When we tell you the truth, you know it as such despite your prior view of reality. Truth is a simple thing, yet for some impossible to accept. Unconditional love is all there is. To find truth, one must find oneself. Finding oneself, you find God. I have only one truth to teach, and that is love. Growth involves reaching an ever-expanding state of love, and with that you will flow with the divine plan of the universe. The way to God is through your inner being."

Leaving the dimension, my being was filled with the love and power of Jesus. Realizing that he represented what I could become, I vowed to myself to continue my journey into light!

I had begun a new threshold of awareness. The goal I sought was to find the true Christ which is within myself, my higher self. A journey had begun, and there were many more pathways to unfold in finding the knowledge that would bond the spirit to the form. . .in a reunion of totality that would unite the eternal understanding of my truest soul to that small part of me that chose to visit this world of fragmentary limitation.

Who was Christ? When he said to all of us that we would do all that he did and more, which direction was he pointing?

In my mind's eye, I saw him. He was pointing towards life. "Seek the life!" he said. "And you will find the truth."

MY MESSAGE TO YOU:

IF YOU NEVER EXPERIENCE ASTRAL TRAVEL, THAT IS OKAY. THE MESSAGE IN MY EXPERIENCE IS THAT WHATEVER PATH YOU TAKE, IT IS GOOD. WHATEVER YOU MAY FEAR, IT IS ILLUSION. AND WHEREVER YOU MAY GO, GOD GOES WITH YOU. ALL THERE IS, IS LOVE!

HAMPTON ROADS
PUBLISHING COMPANY, INC.

Books for the body . . .

Health

Beauty

Nutrition

Books for the mind . . .

Fiction

History

Psychology

Parapsychology

Current Events

Books for the spirit . . .

Spiritual

Inspirational

"New Age"

Would you like to be notified as we publish new books in your area of interest? Would you like a copy of our latest catalog? Fill in this page (or copy it, if you would prefer to leave this book uncut), and send to:

Hampton Roads Publishing Co., Inc
891 Norfolk Square
Norfolk, VA 23502

[__] Please send latest catalog

[__] Please add me to the following mailing list(s):

    [__] Books for the body

    [__] Books for the mind

    [__] Books for the spirit

NAME_____

ADDRESS_____

CITY_____ STATE ___ ZIP_____